Please ...
Don't Tailgate
the Real Estate!

Other Books by the author

Please ...
Don't Tailgate
the Real Estate!

SCOUTING THE BACK ROADS

AND OFF RAMPS TO FIND

TRUE LOVE AND HAPPINESS

William C. Anderson

TRAILER LIFE BOOKS

Production Coordinator: Robert S. Tinnon
Copy Editor: Rena Copperman
Cover Illustration: Bob MacMahon
Cover, Interior Design, and Typesetting: Robert S. Tinnon

This book was set in Stempel Garamond and Adobe Nueva

Printed and bound in the United States of America.

9 8 7 6 5 4 3 2 1

ISBN:0-934798-51-6

To The Dirty Dozen
(and you know who you are)

A deep debt of gratitude to Earl and Gail Bellamy,
Al and Jeannie Clatworthy, Curt and Helen Conklin,
Chuck and Lorie Lenfest,
and Bud and Ginger Shinn

No alliances forged in combat are stronger than those
formed by fellow vagabonds during RVing expeditions.
From Cabo San Lucas, Mexico, to Chicken, Alaska, it has
been our good fortune to have shared hors d'oeuvres and
holding tanks with these comrades in arms.

This journal is dedicated to The Dirty Dozen.
May all their potholes be inverted
and their sewer hoses never whiplash.

Contents

Acknowledgments

Behind every book lurk a lot of characters who are instrumental in seeing the project into fruition. Book designers, copy editors, illustrators, proofreaders—to name a few. Next to the publisher, however, the chief culprit is the editor, a mean-spirited, sadistic individual who wears green eye shades and wields a blue pencil the size of a baseball bat.

Unfortunately, a writer has to be nice to editors, because they are responsible for turning a sow's ear of a manuscript into a silk purse on the bestseller's list. Therefore, I wish to take this opportunity to thank these reluctant heroes who have made gargantuan contributions to this modest offering.

This will take a bit of doing, as the contents of this compendium have been stolen from many sources. First off, I wish to thank the editors of *Reader's Digest* and *Good Housekeeping* for allowing me to plagiarize from books of mine they have condensed. I would like to thank the editors of Crown Publishers, who had the courage to wade through my swill in spite of the sump holes—especially Arthur Fields and Nick Lyons. These two literate gentlemen became so depressed over trying to edit my prose that they set up their own publishing company. Indeed, Nick Lyons and a whippersnapper named Jim Pruett went on to publish the best trout-fishing books in the world.

Much of this omnibus contains my articles from the "Back Roads" and "Off Ramp" columns that have appeared in *MotorHome* magazine. For these assaults on the literary world, a gent named Bill Estes is largely responsible. He spearheads TL

Enterprises, the umbrella for *Trailer Life*, *MotorHome*, and *Highways* magazines. Aside from this hang-up, Bill Estes is a fine figure of a man.

Other editors include Bob Livingston, a hirsute gentleman who has done more for the RV industry than anyone since the inventor of the wheel, and Barbara Leonard, an ingratiating redhead whose consumption of Mylanta® increased three-fold since signing me on. Julia Leigh of *The Retired Officer Magazine* is not only a talented taskmaster but a neat lady; and a doff of my boater to Jim Brightly, a bright young buck who used up so many blue pencils he talked me into switching to computer discs.

A bow to Rick Rundall, one of the nicer managers, who not only runs a tight ship, but came up with the idea of formatting the pages of this book so they will fit neatly in the bottom of an iguana cage.

I'd like to thank my offspring—Ann, Scott, and Holly—for being such patient (if perplexed) participants in our early experiments with RVing. Only now have they learned to heed nature's nudge without first checking the holding tank.

And lastly, a deep bow to Dortha, my long-suffering love, dreamboat, and buddy—who has truly been a copilot above and beyond the pale.

Introduction

Looking back on the mutiny, it is apparent that the Anderson family first became interested in this cockamamie RV lifestyle on the day Scott broke his toilet seat. If our young son hadn't gotten a little behind in his business, all of these awesome adventures would never have occurred. But how was one to know that an innocent sojourn with one's son through the local Sears store in search of the toilet-seat department would trigger a phenomenon of such devastating proportions.

"Hey, Pop, look at these," said my thirteen-year-old ankle-biter as we made the mistake of threading our way through the camping equipment on the way to the plumbing department. Scott was pointing at some sleeping bags alluringly displayed in an idyllic setting in the camping-goods department. "Just what we need for that overnight camping trip you promised us up on Skyline Drive."

The sickening vision of spending a night in a sleeping bag swam before my eyes. I needed an overnight camping trip in a sleeping bag like I needed another appendix. I managed to keep a stiff upper lip until we got home, and then, as in all moments of crisis, I ran to my wife and sobbed out the whole miserable story into her bosom.

"Why, that's grand," said the missus. "By all means let him buy a sleeping bag. You buy one too. A father and son should get out together and commune with Mother Nature. Bond. Get to know your son."

"I already know my son," I said. "I can pick him out in a very large crowd. Have you ever slept in a sleeping bag?"

"Of course not. You know I have claustrophobia."

"I thought so. Nobody sleeps in a sleeping bag, they just spend nights in them."

"Oh? You never saw *For Whom the Bell Tolls?* Gary Cooper slept in one and looked very comfortable when he was leading the fight with the Spanish rebels."

"He was also zipped up with Ingrid Bergman. Under those conditions I would be happy to spend a night—"

"Good fathers must make sacrifices for their children."

"I know a guy who was sleeping in a sleeping bag, got struck by lightning, and it fused his zipper shut. He never could get out of it. He made his living playing mummy roles in Grade B horror movies—"

I received a pat on the cheek. "You told our son you'd take him camping. So take him camping already."

This ultimatum led to Phase One. Which involved another trip to Sears, this time with the family. "How do you like it?" I asked Dortha, pointing at the two-wheeled camper in the sporting-goods section. "Folds out into a nice tent, sleeps four, and there's a stove and icebox. It also has mattresses. On which to sleep. No sleeping bags."

The memsahib looked at the camper curiously. "Where's the bathroom?"

"Bathroom?" I looked at her in disbelief. "Of course there's no bathroom."

"Not even a potty?"

I looked around to see if anyone else was listening. "Of course no potty," I said under my breath.

"No sale."

Phase Two of the campaign involved a trip to the local camper sales office. Again with the family. "Look at that little jewel," I said, pointing at the shiny new camper perched on the back of a pickup truck. "Ain't she a beaut? Sleeps four. Or eight in love. All tucked away comfy and cozy in a little aluminum cocoon."

The missus appraised the aluminum cocoon critically for a moment before wrinkling her nose. "Where's the bathroom?"

"Step in," I said cheerily. "Look at the cute little stove, refrigerator, bunk beds with mattresses. Ice for my martinis while you fix din—"

"Where's the bathroom?" she asked, stepping gingerly into the tiny confines.

"See this cute little sink? You pump water up with this little handle here—"

"Is this the bathroom?" She opened a closet door by the refrigerator.

"That's a closet, dear. But I suppose in a pinch you could—"

"No sale."

Phase Three of the campaign required an agonizing reappraisal of the situation. It was especially agonizing when considering the alternative of spending a night in a sleeping bag. This phase involved a trip to a travel-trailer agency.

Parked sedately in the rear of the lot, it looked like the White House on wheels. Its aluminum skin threw back the sun's rays with a brilliance that dazzled; its welcome mat beckoned to the nattily decored interior with the blue and gold curtains. It was magnificence on rollers. It was a perambulating dream. I ushered my better half into its sumptuousness.

"Well, " said the distaff, her eyes assuming platter proportions as she surveyed the luxury. "This is what I call camping."

"Here's the stove, the fridge, the sink"—then, like Michelangelo unveiling his Pietà, I threw back the shower curtain—"and voilà! A shower and a john. Howzabout that?"

"Does the john flush?"

"The john flushes."

"Tell the nice man we'll take it."

And thus nearly four decades of RVing were launched—all because my son busted a toilet seat.

Our three house apes grew up with a succession of RVs: a travel trailer and three motorhomes. The latter the progeny named after Rocinante, Don Quixote's noble steed on which he rode to strange and wondrous places.

Herewith is a compilation of some of these strange and wondrous journeys, as well as some of the fascinating people Rocinante encountered on her travels. Join us as we do some plain and fancy windmill jousting—the RV way.

You may leave your sleeping bag at home.

WILLIAM C. ANDERSON

Christening Rocinante

The wife gave me the look. "Roomie," she said, "you're out of your skull. You christen babies. And ships. You do not christen motorhomes."

"Of course, you do, mon chère. Do you want our new baby to go out into the world unnamed and unsanctified like a bastard child? Now, I've worked out a little program here for the christening ceremonies. . . ."

"What christening ceremonies?"

"We'll invite a few friends over. Keep it simple. A few 'horses' duffers'—maybe a touch of the tokay."

"A few friends? How many's a few friends?"

I cleared my throat. "I've made a little list here. Comes to about fifty. As I say, we'll keep it simple.

"Fifty."

Sometimes wives can be very difficult. "We'll stagger the invitations. Half can come from 2 to 4, the other half from 4 to . . ."

"Fifty people in our new motorhome? You've had a lot of bird-brained ideas, luv, but this wins the cut-glass flyswatter. Look, let's just pretend we're having a party. I'll make a few cigarette burns on the furniture and stop up the john with cocktail napkins, and we can accomplish the same thing without having to go through the agony."

"My pet, we have no choice. Let me show you something." I produced a small package wrapped in tissue paper. "Our buddies brought this over this afternoon."

With spousely suspicion, she took the package and gingerly unwrapped it. She held a shiny piece of engraved metal up to the light. "What is it?"

"It's a plaque that goes over the door of our new motorhome. The gang had it engraved." Choking back a lump in my throat, I took it from her and held it up over the door. ROCINANTE blinked back in large block letters.

We'd selected the name in honor of Don Quixote's horse. What could be a better sobriquet for a sturdy steed that is going to take us to unchartered lands?

"OK, party boy," she said, rising from her chair. "So we're stuck with a motorhome-christening party. Now if you'll excuse me, I'll start whipping up canapes for fifty people."

"That's my gal." I gave her a playful spank on the bottom. "I knew you'd go for the idea."

The logistics of setting up a bar in the motorhome that would support fifty sets of elbows proved a real challenge, but my solution was brilliant in its simplicity. One of the joys of our new rig is a freshwater tank that holds sixty gallons. Pouring the case of vodka into the tank presented no problem, nor did adding the vermouth, as the eyedropper squirted easily into the tank. Only icing the martinis created a slight dilemma, which was solved by covering the tank (located under the bed) with a gunnysack containing fifty pounds of ice. With a flick of the switch, the water pump was on and a delicious cold, dry martini could be drawn from any tap in the motorhome.

We added a carton of paper cups, a gallon of olives, and a box of toothpicks, and the bar was in business. Here I must admit to one tactical error. Paper cups and alcohol soon develop an incompatibility that results in soggy neckties and slippery bosoms. As it turned out, however, this was one of our more minor problems.

It started out beautifully. Dortha had the yummy hors d'oeu-vres tastefully laid out on the dinette, the smell of fresh-cut roses filled the air, the martinis were cold and sprang to the touch of the tap. Arriving promptly, especially since free booze was involved, our friends quickly began filling the motorhome. The first two hours went swimmingly.

Come four o'clock, however, it was evident my plan wasn't working. The two o'clock contingent dutifully said goodbye, thanked us for a nice party, then got a fresh cup and went back to the martini tap in the bathroom sink—quickly giving credence to the old adage that the only thing worse than a party at which no one shows up is a party at which no one goes home.

Packing fifty people into a motorhome is one way to get to know people. Really get to know people. Among other things, I was startled to discover that one of the wives actually wore a whalebone corset, a commodity I thought had retired with the celluloid collar. It was even more surprising to discover that one generously endowed secretary, whom I had long admired from a distance, turned out to be composed largely of foam rubber.

As interesting as these observations were, they paled by com-parison with the dilemma of our neighborhood clergyman, whose suspenders broke. Trying to pull up his pants, he got his face slapped by three different women and then, tired of being assaulted, he finally abandoned recovery operations and spent the rest of the evening standing around in a pair of loud check-ered shorts.

When the next-door neighbor brought in his wife and twin Dalmations, I began having pangs of concern about the ability of the motorhome shocks to withstand the weight of some four tons of martini swillers. Remedial action obviously was called for.

"Everybody out," I said. "Bobby Tilley is going to chris-ten the motorhome."

Bobby Tilley was the wife of my old boss, Colonel Reade Tilley, whom I had worked with at the Pentagon. Historically, bosses' wives are not the type of people you'd normally clasp to your bosom. Not so with Bobby Tilley. A very ingratiating female, she had wormed her way into our hearts when first we met in Germany during the Berlin Airlift. As honest and without guile as a Paris *pissoir*, in her ample bosom she carries a heart the size of a Volkswagen. Contrary to all established rules, we are very fond of my old boss's wife.

"Everybody out here," she said, squeezing out of the motorhome. "We're going to hit this thing over the nose with a bottle of champagne."

At the sight of the champagne, the revelers squirted out of the rig like unplugged toothpaste. They gathered around as Bobby took a beribboned bottle and poised it over the front bumper. "Are the photographers ready?"

"Ready!" chorused the troops, Polaroids poised.

"Then here goes!" She lifted the bottle over her head. "I christen thee ROCINANTE!" She wound up like a discus thrower, and a haymaker whistled through the air.

Fortunately it was not a major artery. Once we got the compress in place, the blood flow was reduced to a barely noticeable trickle. "I wonder why this never happens to presidents' wives who christen ships," moaned Bobby.

"Probably," her husband said, "because they don't haul off and rap them like they're trying to fell an ox. You damned near caved in the front end of this thing."

"A thing worth doing," she muttered through blue lips, "is worth doing well."

The party had no sooner reconvened inside the motorhome than there was a speedy exodus by an irate young man with

wife in tow. "Best party in years," he grumbled at his struggling spouse, "and you have to pick this time to have the baby!"

The party finally broke up at 3 A.M. with considerable assistance from the distaff and the men of the 82nd Fire Brigade.
There were a few embarrassments as the guests were uncorked
and came tumbling out, not the least of which was our rev-
erend, who, exposed pantless, ran around trying to explain to
everyone that his suspenders had broken and he was not a TV
evangelist on the prowl.

And so it came to pass that Rocinante had suffered innu-
merable indignities plus a possible hernia of the shocks and
would carry the scars of numerous cigarette burns forever. And
there was a good chance of a hysterectomy if the plumber's
friend did not relieve a blockage of the commode created by a
size 7 party shoe that had somehow gotten flushed down. Fortunately, as far as we could tell, no one was wearing it.

But the soiree had been an unqualified success—a blockbuster
of the first magnitude. Our new acquisition was not about to
be thrust out into the world an unnamed, unsanctified, bastardly
child. Our new baby had been properly christened!

On Naming
Your Motorhome

It seems everyone has a pet name for their motorhome. We've all heard fascinating handles roaming our CB airwaves, from Shasta (Shasta have lots of gas and oil!) to Wheel Estate, The Tiltin' Hilton to The Perambulatin' Parlor. Americans not only like to name things, but in our CB traveling fraternity, a handle for our RV is a necessity.

However, a recent encounter with an RVer who had a problem with the naming of his rig underscores the importance of giving a lot of thought to the sobriquet bestowed upon one's toddling townhouse.

We were plugging into Benbow Valley RV Resort near Garberville, in the heart of Northern California's redwood empire. Not only does this beautiful park have all the usual amenities nestled in the lap of splendiferous scenery, but it also boasts a nifty nine-hole golf course, complete with pro shop.

I was hooking up the park's cable television (I can remember when an RV park was considered luxurious if it were not festooned with cowpies) when a burly gentleman pulled up in his golf cart.

"That Dolphin's a nice-lookin' rig," said the man, surveying my latest acquisition.

"We're very happy with it," I said, looking into the face of the golfer. I was glad to see his sunburned countenance was split by an easy grin, as his tattooed forearms bore the girth of telephone poles.

"Rocinante," he said, reading the name lettered on the tire cover. "That what you call your rig?"

"Right. We named it after Don Quixote's horse."

"Why?"

"Good question. Rocinante carried Quixote into strange and distant lands. Our rig does the same thing, and the wife and I do a lot of windmill tilting."

He squeezed his eyes at me. "Weird. But it beats the hell out of the name we call our rig."

"What's that?"

"Hanky Panky."

"Hanky Panky?"

"Yep. Ain't that a lulu?"

"Hanky Panky. Nothing wrong with that. I've heard a lot worse names for an RV."

"No, you ain't. You got no idea the problems that name has given me. For instance, you ever tried to get a license for an RV named Hanky Panky?"

"No," I said, tightening up the cable connection. "So what's the problem?"

"Well, it started the first day we got the rig. I live in Beaumont, Texas. I called the nearest branch of the Department of Motor Vehicles and asked the sweet young thing how I went about getting a license for Hanky Panky. Know what she said?"

"No."

"She said you need a license for dogs, marriage, and huntin' moose, but as far as she knew, you didn't need a license for hanky-panky. I told her I would get arrested if I didn't have a license for Hanky Panky. She said, 'Well, if they've passed a law requiring a license for hanky-panky in Texas, it sure should bring in a lot of revenue.'"

"Hold it," I said. "You're not laying on me the old classic about the man with a dog named Sex, and the problems he had trying to get a license."

His right hand shot up. "No way. That's only part of the story. You should have heard the rhubarb I had getting the rig insured. I called my insurance agent and said, 'I want to insure Hanky Panky.' Know what he said?"

"No," I said.

"He said, 'Don't we all?' Didn't take long to realize that conversation was goin' nowhere. Especially when I told him I wanted to insure my Hanky Panky against lawsuits, collision, and earthquakes.

"He said he didn't know what kind of kinky club I belonged to, but he'd sure like to join up."

"It appears that you may indeed have picked a troublesome nickname for your rig."

"I didn't pick it. My wife did. She said that now that I had retired, there'd be more time for Hanky Panky. I got all excited until I found out that's what she'd named the Winnebago."

He sighed. "It sure ain't been easy. Like when I checked in here. Shouldn't be all that complicated. All I asked when I signed in was, 'Do you have a place for Hanky Panky?' That pretty little filly at the counter said, 'You kidding? We don't even have a place for a coffee break.'"

"I see what you mean."

"Took half an hour to get that conversation back on track."

"One never knows what a simple act like naming one's motorhome can lead to."

"That's for dang sure. I won't even tell you about the time I had to go traffic court when I got a ticket for having Hanky Panky in a tow-away zone."

"Thanks. I'd rather not hear about it," I replied.

"Or the time I tried to talk a garage mechanic into giving my Hanky Panky a tune-up."

"Please!" I held up my hands. "Enough already." I stowed my tool chest and turned to the golfer. "I've finished hooking up. Can I buy you a cold drink?"

"No, thanks. Gotta be off." He started his golf cart. "Didn't mean to bore you with my tales of Hanky Panky."

"No problem. I found your experiences with Hanky Panky very enlightening."

"Well, my troubles will soon be over. We're changing the name of our rig; no more hassles."

"Makes sense. What's going to be the new name of your Winnebago?"

He accelerated his golf cart, and as it headed down the road, he shot it over his shoulder: "Sex Hour. How does that grab ya'?"

"Now that's a name!" I shouted after him, trying it on for size. "Sex Hour."

"Gracious," said a comely young lady sticking her head out of the Vogue parked in the next site. "Is it that time already?"

Barging in on Old Buddies

Among the many virtues of owning our own little peripatetic parlor is the fantastic flexibility it affords us worshippers of the wanderlust. For instance, when one finds oneself in the neighborhood of old friends and wants to drop in unannounced, if driving one's own self-contained condo, an unexpected visitation may be made with a minimum of vexation.

This is best illustrated by a cross-country motorhome trip that took us through Mississippi. This Southern-fried state might be a bit shorthanded in its public relations tubthumping department, which is a shame, for it needs to take a backseat to no real estate when it comes to scenic beauty.

The drive along Mississippi's Gulf Coast is a panorama of gorgeous beaches, fishing villages, coastal resorts, and antebellum history that staggers the senses. Approaching Biloxi, we couldn't resist the temptation to check out this beguiling city. We spurred Rocinante off on a side trip to cruise through town.

Exuding Old World dignity, Biloxi is one of the largest shrimp- and oyster-packing centers in America. It also has the good sense to blanket this potential olfactory problem with masses of magnolia, crepe myrtle, dogwood, camellias, and azaleas. As a result, one whiffs not the pungent but the poetic.

Galloping on to Ocean Springs, Rocinante let it be known that it was time for the vistas of sun-kissed waters in the Gulf to be replaced by oat-kissed chow in her nose bag. I turned to my copilot, "Spouse, our trusty steed is flagging. Howzabout a heading for the nearest barn?"

"Ocean Springs," ruminated the redhead, picking up the campground directory. "I just happen to remember. We have old friends who live here. You remember the Evanses, Jack and La Verne?"

"Of course! We haven't seen them in a century. They now live in Ocean Springs?"

"They do. Let's give them a call. They can probably recommend a good campground."

Pulling into a gas station, I refueled and used the phone. "Anderson?" came a booming voice over the wire. "You the weenie that's married to that pretty redhead?"

"The same. We just happened to be in the neighborhood. Thought you might like to buy us a drink."

"You mean you're here in town?"

"Affirmative."

"Well for goodness sake, get your mangy carcass out here."

"Will do. But first we gotta find a stable for Rocinante." I explained that we were in our motorhome and were looking for a place to park for the night. "I thought we might park on one of these nice sandy beaches."

"Not tonight. The Hell's Angels are in town. They drink coffin shellac and do weird things."

"Like what weird?"

"Like last night. A guy went to bed in his trailer gassed to the gills and woke up this morning to find his rig floating out in the Gulf. Pranksters had towed his trailer down to the dock and launched it. The poor slob stepped out to go to the john and fell into thirty fathoms of water."

"I don't believe it."

"Neither did the drunk. Especially when he was arrested by

the Coast Guard for being a threat to maritime navigation. What you're gonna do is get your highway hacienda out to our house on the double. Put Dortha on and I'll give her directions. You couldn't find your fanny with both hands."

Service life creates a lot of friendships. I had known Jack Evans since the days of the B-36 and the battleship, and we had even served a tour together at Fort Fumble, as he lovingly called the Pentagon. As a result, the likable naval aviator and his gracious southern wife, La Verne, had become a cornerstone when Dortha and I started cementing service relationships.

Evans guided us onto his driveway like a meatball directing landings on an aircraft carrier, positioned us precisely, and slid his fingers across his throat. I cut the engine.

He came bounding into the coach and scooped up Dortha in a big bear-hug. "My little dove," he cooed into her ear, "I always knew you'd fly to me on the wings of love. But why did you have to bring old Goatbreath?"

"He's just the driver," said the distaff.

"Outstanding." He turned to me. "We have water and electrical hookups, but afraid we don't have a sewer outlet. Knowing you, that's probably the prime requirement."

"We're completely self-contained, swabbie. Don't need a thing. And speaking of containers," I patted his midriff. "I see you're now carrying your bowling ball in your skivvies."

He patted his tummy. "Something you air force zoomies know nothing about. We navy types believe in carrying a little ballast. Makes for a smoother ride through choppy seas." He peered through the windshield and swept the vista with his hand. "Now, how's that for a view?"

Dortha whistled as we looked out over a rolling acreage of clipped grass bracketed by tall cypresses. "Wow! That is some backyard."

"It also happens to be an eighteen-hole golf course. I think you'll be comfortable. But, come. The sun is setting over the yardarm. Let's hie to the bar."

We toasted the yardarm in the Evans's handsome southern home. No slouch as a host, Evans was ably abetted by La Verne, who kept passing around heaping platters of the best fresh shrimp that ever surrendered to a toothpick.

"Jack," I asked, "when you retired from the navy, how did you happen to settle in Ocean Springs, Mississippi?"

"You remember our last tour at Disneyland East. Well, if Pentagon duty wasn't bad enough, we had to put up with that miserable Shirley Highway. In a snowstorm, that blasted road gave me more ulcers than riding typhoons in a destroyer. So when I hung up the suit, I told La Verne we were heading south. Along the way we'd keep asking service station attendants if they had any antifreeze. When we found a place that answered with 'What's antifreeze?' that's the place we'd plant roots. It just happened to be Ocean Springs."

Following the attitude adjustment hour, we tooted off to Jack's favorite eatery, a restaurant that served Cajun heartburn. It was prepared by an ebullient French chef who would accompany each course to the table, then purse his lips, kiss a cluster of fingers, throw them to the ceiling, and shout, "Ambrosia. Nectar of the Gods!"

The gastronomic fires were quenched with a slice of peanut-butter cream pie, then it was back to the Evanses for a cup of Jack's famous Spanish coffee.

Evans' brew is more a ritual than a beverage, as he goes through an Oscar-winning performance of grinding the coffee beans, turning brandy and sugar in a huge snifter over a brandy warmer until it ignites, then adding the coffee together with a huge scoop of whipped cream.

While I stood guard with the fire extinguisher, he mixed up a batch with only one minor explosion. I'd never admit it under the most excruciating torture, but this navy swab makes the world's greatest coffee.

Gorged with delicious food and grog, the women finally peeled off, leaving Evans and me to rehash the wars by ourselves. It was well into the wee hours when our inner fires began to fade with the flame in the brandy warmer, and we finally had to heed the voices from the distaffs summoning us to the feathers.

The next morning we hosted our hosts for breakfast in the rig, then we were on our way without so much as dirtying the guest towels of our visitees.

As we passed through Pascagoula the next morning, we rehashed the great evening. "I hate to admit it," I said, "but those navy types really know how to roll out the red carpet."

"That they do," agreed Dortha, patting Rocinante on the dash. "And thanks to our little housebroken beauty here, we didn't even spot the rug."

An interesting postscript to this story: the Evanses became so infected with our lifestyle that they recently bought a motorhome and are heading this way.

Anyone have a recipe for Spanish coffee?

Baker's Acres

The members of our free-wheeling fraternity are as varied and unique as the rigs they drive, all of which adds to the charm of RVing. Some high-on-the-hoggers never venture out without reservations at a posh campground offering no less than a sauna, an olympic-sized pool, and an eighteen-hole golf course. At the other end of the spectrum lie the pothole-dodgers, who are as interested in the trip as they are in the destination. To them, getting there is more than half the fun. Big Red and I plead guilty to belonging to both groups. We like a nice park if we plan to spend some time at a destination; we also like to head out with only a vague objective in mind, moseying along, sniffing the garlic, and rooting around in the the grass roots.

We were happily indulging ourselves in the latter lifestyle in central Texas, when we pulled into Fort Stockton to gas up. Refreshed, Rocinante kicked up her heels and we headed east out of town to gobble up a few more miles before the salubrious hour set in. We tackled another hour's worth of real estate before the ennui of staring at scrub brush and milo maize began to take its toll.

We reined Rocinante off the freeway and onto a country road that led into a small town. Spotting a gas station surrounded by a lot of empty space that looked inviting, we turned in and pulled up to the pumps. As I shut off the engine, a young, skinny stack of acne came bouncing up.

"Yes, sir. Fill 'er up?"

"Top the tank," I said, tossing him the keys. "And then you get to make a command decision."

"Yes, sir. I get to make a what?"

"A command decision. After you fill the tank you can decide whether to let me park for the night in the back of your station or whether you want to watch me set fire to this motorhome right here. I've been driving all day and I do not intend to take this rig one mile farther tonight."

He inserted the hose and looked up. "Probably wouldn't be a very good idea to set fire to your rig so close to these gas pumps."

"Probably wouldn't."

"Why not park the bus right over there by that little taco stand?"

"Will it be safe?"

"I dunno. But ain't nobody ever stole the taco stand."

"That's good to know."

I paid for the gas, then jockeyed the coach around behind the taco stand. The spot offered a panoramic view of the short-order cook up to his dewlaps in burrito dough. Deciding we could probably beat this scenic vista, I pulled out to search for the local cemetery, which usually afforded much nicer surroundings. As we poked through the village, Dortha spied a hand-scrawled sign in front of a vacant lot reading OVERNIGHTERS WELCUM. I slowed to look it over.

As I did so, a man came bounding out onto the street, waving his hat. With a grand flourish, he motioned us onto the lot. After giving the wife a dubious glance, I swung onto the driveway. I no sooner stopped than the short, rotund man came puffing up to the driver's window. "Name's Sam Baker," he said, bowing to the missus and wadding his hat in his hands. "Welcome to Baker's Acres."

I looked around. The place was hardly lush, but it did have some grass and trees, and it was off the street. "Nice place you have here," I said.

"Just opened up," said Mr. Baker.

"I see. How about amenities?"

"Amenities?" His brow puckered. "Got no amenities. Everybody here's as friendly as can be."

"Good. Then how about hookups?"

He beamed. "You bet. Got everything. Including cable television."

"No kidding? And what do you charge for all this largesse?"

"Five dollars. That includes the cable television."

"Five bucks a night?"

His face clouded. "Does seem like a lot of money. Is it too much?"

Dortha smiled at him. "We'll scrape it up, Mr. Baker."

His face lit up again. "Then you just swing into that space yonder, under that tree. Need any help hooking up?"

"No thanks," I said. "We'll manage."

"Good. When you're all hooked up, just drop into the office and register." The little leprechaun disappeared.

"Isn't he adorable!" gushed the redhead as I put the coach in gear.

"Adorable," I said, "is hardly the word."

The hookups were rustic but adequate. After plugging in, Dortha and I went in search of Mr. Baker's office. We finally located it under a tree. A scrawled placard nailed to a tree above a card table attested to that fact. Mr. Baker saw us coming and turned a sign around on the table reading from CLOSED to OPEN.

"Nice office," I said, handing him a bill.

He took the money and pointed to a dog-eared diary on the card table. "Would you kindly sign the register?" As I complied, he added, "It's a nice office. Air-conditioned. Only trouble is, the pesky squirrels keep eating my register book. You folks hooked up all right?"

"Fine. But there's one small problem with the water bib. Sends out a spray of water when you turn it on."

"Don't worry none about that. That's how I water the grass. Notice how green things is? Once in a while the sewer backs up, and that helps, too."

"I see." I gave the wife a nervous look.

"I play the violin," said Mr. Baker. "You folks like violin music?"

"Love it," said Dortha, before I could kick her in the shins.

"Good. Sometimes we have a little hoedown around here. Luke, he's my neighbor, plays the harmonica. Say, would you like us to play for you folks tonight?"

I broke the pencil signing the register. "That would sure be nice, Mr. Baker," I said, "but that would be quite an imposition. It's been a long day, so we'll probably just eat and turn in early."

"Good. We'll be over about seven o'clock."

As it turned out, Mr. Baker's violin only had three strings, which was more teeth than Luke had, and the highly touted cable television had only one station. But whatever one might say about Texans—and there has been plenty said—no one can deny their hospitality. Some, according to the wife, are even adorable. As we left Baker's Acres the next morning, I made a thorough inspection of the rig to be sure Dortha hadn't smuggled the little elf aboard.

In sum, there is a definite place for posh resort campgrounds. But the parking spots that really add pepperoni to our peregrinating pizza are the ones out in the boonies. Off the beaten path.

For until one has heard "I'll Meet You in the Henhouse, Helen, If You Will Egg Me On" rendered by a three-stringed violin and a toothless harmonica player, one has not truly lived.

Motorhoming
Is for the Birds

Washed by ocean breezes, Guadalupe, California, is a clean, snoozing, agricultural town just north of Vandenberg Air Force Base. Its main claims to fame are three: the Far Western Steak House, which serves the best hunk of beef in the Northern Hemisphere; the site where Cecil B. DeMille filmed *The Ten Commandments*; and an ebullient, pretty schoolteacher known as the "Bird Lady of Guadalupe."

On a recent visit to this backroads town, we had plugged Rocinante into one of the many splendiferous RV parks that dot the area and were entertaining the Bird Lady, also known as Holly Anderson. Sweet of breath, auburn of hair, and bountiful of brisket, Holly was wiping the dishes after a sumptuous dinner Big Red had prepared in the rig.

"It's strictly for the birds," said Holly, looking around the coach as she scrubbed a pan.

I looked at her quizzically. "What's for the birds?"

"Motorhomes. Definitely for the birds."

"I thought you liked our trundling townhouse."

"I do. It's fantastic. That's why it's for the birds. They'd love it too."

The light came on. Holly had acquired her nickname because her hobby was raising birds. During a visit to her house, we had seen birds in every room, including the john. Hundreds of birds. Were they all to become airborne at the same time, the whole house could well go flapping south for the winter. "You mean an RV would be a fitting habitat for a bird?"

"Of course. Birds are very intelligent. They like to travel around, see new sights, eat new foods. . . ."

"Poop on the furniture."

"Hold on. What about cats and dogs? Cats have to have a smelly old litter box. You have to follow a dog around with a pooper-scooper. . . ."

"Exactly. That's why Big Red and I own guppies."

"I'm not knocking goldfish. Or four-legged pets. But a bird is a perfect pet for RVers. Especially fulltimers. Let me lay something on you." She tapped my nose with a soapy forefinger. "Take cats. They're very aloof. They have one claim to fame: they can curl up in your lap and purr. When they're not in the mood to claw the furniture."

"Dogs are different. They're man's best friend."

"If you like to follow your best friend around with a pooper-scooper, listen to barking all night, and pick its hair out of your granola. Have you ever noticed that the smaller the RV, the bigger the dog that lives in it?" She motioned out the window. "See that pop-up camper over there with the Saint Bernard tied to it? The first cat that comes by, those campers will find their home in the next county."

"You don't buy an RV to accommodate your pet."

"No. What I'm saying is, maybe you should get a pet that would be suitable to your RV. A bird can greet you by name when you come home. They can be potty trained, and they don't require walks in the middle of the night. There are no leash or poop-scoop laws for birds. They talk to you when you're lonely. They dance, laugh, perform tricks, bathe often, amuse you with their comical antics, and they love you unconditionally."

"Lots of people have dogs for protection. Cops say a dog is one of the best crime deterrents there is."

"Granted. But if you get a talking bird, you can teach it to bark. One bird owner I know has taught her African grey parrot to say, 'Hey, Sam, let out the pit bull!' when it hears a strange noise. How about that for deterrence?"

I found I was being intrigued by this bird banter. "What kind of bird would you buy for an RV?"

"Well, for a small, low-maintenance bird, finches or canaries are nice. They come in many colors. Male canaries sing up a storm."

"How about a little larger model?"

"Then we're talking parakeets, cockatiels, lovebirds. . . . One of my favorites is the conure. The sun and jenday conures make beautiful pets; they're loving and clownish. The smaller green-cheeked or maroon-bellied conures have personalities that would win over the heart of an anvil."

"I used to have a secretary who was a bobbing-breasted clock-watcher. . . ."

"If you want a bird that can hold its own with the family cat, I'd recommend several: the African grey is a delightful companion and can quote Shakespeare; the amazon has beautiful coloration and is highly intelligent; minimacaws are playful and loving; and cockatoos want to be petted all day long. Bigger birds, of course, require more space. When you buy your bird, try to get one that's been hand-fed. They tend to be sweeter and more affectionate."

"I wasn't planning on buying a bird."

"Do it." She smiled. "They'll love your guppies."

"For lunch. So you think a bird would be happy in the close confines of an RV?"

"Definitely. As much as any other pet. A bird should be in its cage when alone. Wings should be clipped. Lightweight birds like cockatiels and parakeets can shoot out the door, and it's bye-bye birdie. If the bird is taken outside to share the scenery, it should be kept in its cage. That way it will be protected from stray cats, barking dogs, and love-starved pouter pigeons on the prowl.

"One word of caution, however. Remember when coal miners sent canaries into the mine shafts to sample the air? Birds have very sensitive respiratory systems. So overheating Teflon or non-stick pans, drip pans on stoves, waffle irons, or other cookware creates deadly fumes that, in the closed area of an RV, could kill a bird. So the RV should be aired out when using sprays. Open pots of soup or grease should be covered, and toilet lids should be kept closed. That's about it. Just common sense."

"I always thought that birds were messy. They have the eating habits of a teenager."

"Not necessarily. Most seed-eating birds can be converted to a pelleted diet. Pellets come in all shapes, colors, and flavors, specifically formulated for the type of bird you have. They provide a balanced nutritional diet—a vast improvement over seeds.

"Most anything that's good for you is good for your bird. And there's an interesting bonus." She reached over and patted the midriff that used to be my chest. "Some bird owners, in providing healthy foods for their pets, find themselves changing their own diets—cutting out junk food and sweets. Offering your bird fresh fruit and veggies will make for a healthier bird. Not to mention the bird owner."

"This info could be of interest to our legions of RVers. If anyone wants more info on birds and RVs, could they give you a call?"

"Of course. My e-mail address is hollyanderson@74031,414. I'll be happy to answer any questions after work."

For not only is Holly known as the "Bird Lady of Guadalupe," she's also known as our daughter. If she doesn't cooperate, we'll send her to the naughty chair.

The Motorhome:
A Many-Splendored Thing

"Is the checklist complete?" I asked the copilot as I buckled up the seat belt of Rocinante, our bouncing bunkhouse.

"Yes, luv," said the redhead, crawling into the copilot's seat. She held up her hand and started ticking off her fingers. "Our Five-P checklist is complete: We have our special Pillows, Pills, Prunes, Pajamas, and Poothtaste. Everything we need. Roll 'em!"

All of us lucky rat-race refugees know that one of life's greatest pleasures is to slide behind the wheel in our motorized mansion, start the engine, and, whiffing the aroma of fresh-brewed coffee, head out of the driveway to joust with the unknown delights of the open road.

It is this serendipitous sense of freedom, adventure, and wanderlust that has captivated Americans, increasing the popularity of recreational vehicles to where one out of every four families now has a getaway conveyance of some sort. All of this is, of course, no news to our free-wheeling fraternity of motorhome aficionados.

But what may not be as well known are the many uses toddling townhouses are now being called upon to perform in addition to their recreational duties. If the mail to the "Off Ramp" column is any indication, our motorhomes are being employed for many more purposes than were originally conceived by their manufacturers. Cases in point:

Emergency Ward: There is nothing handier than having a motorhome pull up to the scene of an accident. Recently a couple of Idahoans imprudently flew their light plane into a power line. Fortunately, their plane crashed in the desert along U.S. 95. A family in their Winnebago came upon the crash site, turned their RV into an emergency ward, and supplied beds and emergency equipment for the wounded. The injured pilot was extricated from the airplane with the aid of the tool kit carried in the motorhome.

With increasing frequency, motorhomers are lauded for providing succor and supplies in disaster situations. Good Sam Club members are truly becoming Good Samaritans by virtue of not only having communication facilities but being blessed with life-saving equipment ranging from fire axes to first-aid kits.

Command Posts: As any survivor of Hurricane Andrew's wrath will be quick to testify, RV owners were generally the luckiest of the lot. While house roofs were flying all over Florida, lucky RVers generally had power, heat, water, and a roof over their heads. More than one RV owner found his rig became the neighborhood command post, thanks to a generator that provided emergency power for radio and television disaster-relief information and a stove that could heat baby bottles.

Motorhomes are also used by insurance and disaster teams as temporary offices in natural-disaster areas to more quickly assess damage and expedite relief aid.

Medical Housing: Hospitals in Salt Lake City, Utah, are typical of the many medical facilities that now provide parking spaces for RVs. The University Regional Medical Center has an RV lot with sixteen spaces with full hookups for $8 a night. Families from outlying states, who have a member attending this excellent facility, may provide the necessary emotional support for their loved ones without being caught in the vice-squeeze of high-priced motels and restaurants.

The knowledge that one's family may be only a few steps away from the hospital has a most salubrious effect on the patient; and when returning a convalescent to his or her home, there is no more comfortable transport in the world than an RV.

Cinematic Caravans: Having experienced firsthand how Hollywood studios can make lousy movies out of good books, I still retain a grudging admiration for the way the production crews employ RVs in making a motion picture. When filming in a remote location, motorhomes are often used to house the stars when no other facilities are available. The grandeur of the motorhome, of course, depends upon the pecking order of the talent. To show the status of the writer, I have been known to sleep in a pop-up trailer just aft of the Porta Potties.

Literally dozens of RVs invade a remote shooting location, providing not only housing, but the wardrobe department; movie prop warehouse; camera, sound, and lighting equipment; food-catering kitchen; makeup salons; and, of course, the honeywagon. And more and more, thanks to the self-contained mobility of the RV, motorhome assignment is often a part of a movie star's contract, even when filming on a movie lot.

Civic Commuters: Many communities have discovered that it's sometimes more convenient to bring the mountain to Mohammed. RVs have been converted to rolling libraries; dentists, doctors, and veterinarians have converted RVs into offices and medical labs; complete banking services have been incorporated into motorhomes; museums and historical artifacts have been showcased in peregrinating exhibits—all to service people in the boondocks and isolated areas.

And the rolling residence has truly proved a boon to engineers, surveyors, and crews who build and maintain highways and railroad beds in areas a zillion miles from nowhere.

Roving Reporters: The multipurpose list of RV users would be incomplete were we to omit the pundits who use an RV in reporting the human condition. Had John Steinbeck never used his camper to roam the country with his dog, Charles, the literary world would be the less for not having the chronicle of his immortal *Travels with Charley*.

And Charles Kuralt's love/hate relationship with the motorhomes in which he prowled America's grass roots is the warp and the woof of the book and TV experiences that were illumined in his marvelous *On the Road* series.

And the list goes on. With their manifold functions that often embrace humanitarian aspects, motorhomers are gradually replacing the position formerly enjoyed by truck drivers as being "Knights of the Road." The old image of an RV as a boxed turtle whose main function was to slow up traffic has been drastically changed. Now, not only do our motorhomes keep up with traffic flow, they also house contents that can be very beneficial to the public and fellow travelers. Indeed, RVs are becoming more and more respected and accommodated.

At least, that's what Sam MacTavish of Beaver Creek, a tiny speed bump in the Yukon, is counting on. He is investing in a 35-foot motorhome, which he plans to convert into a rolling den to house damsels of negotiable virtue. The perambulating "Pasture of Rapture" is designed to cruise the Yukon outposts and bring smiles to the faces of lonely gold prospectors and trappers.

So the next time you see a motorhome with a red light over the door, honk to old Sam. This entrepreneur is really bringing a new meaning to the term "recreational vehicle."

The Storm

I spurred Rocinante off the freeway at Concordia, a snoozing Missouri hamlet just east of Kansas City. The navigator found a nice little oasis complete with roaming tame deer, and we plugged in for the night. We hit the sack early and were soon lulled to sleep by the soothing chomping of the deer eating our welcome mat.

Along about midnight, however, our idyllic snoring was rudely ruptured by a growling, crackling, thunder-clapping electrical storm that sent Dortha to my side of the bed to grip me in a throttling embrace. "I would enjoy this even more, my dear," I croaked, "were your curlers not collapsing my windpipe."

"Sorry," she said, removing her curlers from my throat to plant them in my eye. "But this is a frightening storm. Look at that lightning!"

Raindrops the size of egg yolks began pelting the coach. A bolt struck nearby, flooding the sky with a million klieg lights. "That one did it," I said, noting the night-light was no longer burning. "There goes the power."

She cocked one eyelid at me. "Times like this I appreciate our little aluminum cocoon. We can switch to battery power."

I rolled over. "In the morning. Go back to sleep."

As she cuddled up, we both heard the knock on the door. "Who could be out in the storm this time of night?"

"Best I find out." I slipped into my robe, found the flashlight, and opened the door. The beam illumined a small female figure, clutching a whipping kimono. The woman shielded her face from the spattering rain as she grimaced into the light. "I'm terribly sorry to bother you, sir, but it's a matter of extreme emergency."

"Won't you step in?"

"Thank you, no. This storm has blown out the camp power, and I must switch to our generator. But I can't seem to get it started. Do you know anything about generators?"

"A little." I turned the beam to sweep the outline of a large Superior coach that had driven into a nearby lot during the night. "Is that your motorhome?"

"Yes. And it's absolutely imperative that I get the generator running. Can you help me?"

There was no denying the look of near hysteria in her face. "Of course. I'll get my raincoat."

"Oh, thank you!" She ran back to her coach.

"What is it?" asked Dortha, as I threw on my slicker.

"A damsel in distress. Gotta go."

"What could be so important as to need electricity this time of the night? In this storm?"

"I dunno. But the lady's genuinely worried." I went out the door. "Stay tuned."

I joined the lady huddled over the generator well, trying frantically to get it started. The battery was not cranking the engine. "It might be grounding out because of the rain," I said. "Have you an umbrella?"

"Yes," she said. I noticed she was trembling.

"Get it. And some towels."

"Back in a flash."

I thrust my hand into the spaghetti of wiring. There was a

crackling spit of electricity, and I found myself sitting flat on my butt in the mud. I swore, as the electrical shock left my arm half-numb.

When the woman reappeared with the towels and umbrella, I propped the opened bumbershoot over the generator well to keep out the rain. "I think I've found the problem. The insulation on the wire from the battery has worn off. The naked wire is grounding out. I need some electrical tape."

"Be right back."

Isolating the guilty wire, I wiped it dry. When she returned with the tape, I soon had the wire reinsulated and tucked back into its place. I pressed the starter button. The generator kicked on, and lights began blossoming inside the coach. I turned to the lady to see an immense flood of relief wash over her face. "You're back in business."

She turned her face to mine, the salt of tears mingling with the dripping rain. "How can I ever thank you?"

"You just have. By that expression on your face. But I'm curious to know why it's so dad-blamed important to have your generator going this time of night."

"You're certainly entitled to an explanation. Come with me."

I followed her into the coach. Shaking off the rain, I saw a handsomely appointed interior. Then, the soft whirring sound of machinery caught my ear. Turning toward its source, I did a double take. The forward right side of the rig's furniture had been replaced by a built-in motorized bed. On the bed was a man dressed in pajamas. Over the top of the man's body was a portable respirator, humming with a slight clicking sound. The man smiled up at me.

"Excuse me, neighbor," he said, "for not standing up. Name's Jerry Clark."

"Bill Anderson," I said awkwardly, rehinging my jaw.

"You've met my wife, Virginia. We owe you a large debt, dragging you out on a night like this."

"It was nothing."

"We always plug into a power source at night, and, of course, the generator keeps us in business when we're under way. And we have a battery backup system in case something happens to the generator. But tonight when the storm knocked the main power out, and then the generator wouldn't start, Virginia got upset. She's a worrywart."

"A worrywart, am I?" said Virginia. "That respirator has to do your breathing for you. And it takes a lot of electricity. We don't know for sure how long the backup batteries will last."

"A long time," said Jerry, dismissing the danger.

"Scared me to death." She looked into my eyes. "I want to thank you. You're a lifesaver. Literally."

"No way. But I am curious. I've never seen a lashup quite like this before."

"Nor have very many people," said Jerry, grinning. "I contracted polio when I was forty, spent the usual bout with hospitals and iron lungs until I improved enough to go home with a portable respirator. But being an active lawyer all my life, I got tired of lying around the house. That's when we got the brainstorm and had Superior build us this customized coach. It has saved the day."

"Fantastic!" I said. "So where's home?"

"We're from a little town outside of Portland, Oregon. See this big picture window at bed level? No longer does the world pass me by. I go with it. Go to football games, visit friends, call on clients . . . it's marvelous."

"And Virginia does the driving?"

"Sometimes a friend does. But Virginia hangs in there with the best of 'em. Handles the rig like a truck driver."

I shook my head. "Unbelievable."

Jerry chuckled. "Why? You think a guy should stop living just because he can't breathe?"

"No way! No way should a man stop living!" I gripped his hand. "And now I've puddled your rug long enough. If you have any more problems with your generator, holler. I'll hook mine up to your rig."

"Thanks again, Mr. Anderson." I received an unexpected kiss on the cheek from Virginia as I headed out the door.

"So tell me," said Dortha as I slid back under the covers. "What was that all about?"

I snuggled up to her warmth. "I'll tell you. But first you have to promise me something."

"Anything."

"Promise me that if I ever get to feeling sorry for myself, you'll kick my derriere into the middle of next week."

"That I'll promise. But may I ask why?"

And then I told her about the Clarks from a small town just outside of Portland, Oregon.

The Pilgrimage

Etta Power was a cute little whipstitch, measuring barely five feet from pedal to pate. Although small, she was wound tight—cut from the bolt of the true pioneer. She stoically lost a son to the war, a breast to cancer, and nearly her mind to the vicissitudes of rearing a family of seven in a tiny house with one bathroom.

She dammed four of the orneriest kids who ever snuck a garter snake into a teacher's lunch pail, but for some reason—thanks to the dotings of Etta and her husband, George—her offspring all turned out to be downright respectable. Son Merle was a handsome young buck who never came home from the war in Europe; Otto, a wheeler-dealer, married a pretty Swede and became a millionaire by dealing in real estate.

Of the two girls, daughter Alice was the most vivacious, with beautiful auburn hair and the cutest buns in town, which were no hindrance in helping her snag a successful Colorado publisher named Fred Pruett. Daughter Dortha, a redhead as pretty but not quite as lucky as her sister, ended up sharing the surname, royalties, and trundle bed (not necessarily in that order) of yours truly.

Thus, Etta Power became my mother-in-law. And if one has to have a mother-in-law, I'm glad she was mine. Not only did she make from-scratch chicken-and-noodles, but she could knock off a cobbler made from hand-picked huckleberries that would drool the necktie of the most jaded gourmet. Needless to say, she was deeply loved by all her kids, including her sons-in-law. This, in itself, was no small miracle.

Some years ago a big change started coming over Etta. Her husband was long gone, and a variety of ailments began an attack that even her stout pioneer stock couldn't repel. Now into her nineties, it was quickly becoming apparent that her fighting spirit was beginning to flag.

A family powwow was held. The siblings had already provided the best medical care available and had arranged for a full-time housekeeper. As a result, in spite of being in considerable pain, Etta took it all in stride and comported herself with dignity and good humor.

It was after her thimbleful of blackberry wine one evening that we managed to extract the reason for the wistfulness. Etta wanted to visit her old childhood home before she rocked off to her great reward. Since the lovable matriarch had never asked for a thing in her life, it was forthwith vowed by the family that her wish would be fulfilled at once.

This well-meaning decision soon proved to be fraught with problems. Etta lived in Boise, Idaho, and her childhood home was the old Rock Ranch near Torrington, Wyoming—a distance of some 800 miles. Etta's health required much bed rest, a strict diet, and frequent use of plumbing facilities. This ruled out travel by car, bus, train, or plane.

Then we got the idea. A motorhome would provide everything needed for a safe and pleasant journey for our beloved.

She could stretch out and rest to her heart's content, she would have her own bathroom available upon demand, and her rolling kitchen could be stocked with the requisites needed for her special diet. An ideal solution.

Informed of our decision, the thought that she would be able to visit her old stomping ground brought a new glow to Etta's cheeks and a twinkle in her eyes.

We now had only one problem to overcome: I was between motorhomes at the time, having sold our Apollo while awaiting the delivery of a new Southwind. Rather than risk waiting for the new rig, we elected to rent a motorhome in Boise. Shopping around, we ended up with a nice 27-foot Jamboree, practically new, with all the bells and whistles that would provide a comfortable passage for our VIP.

It was a beautiful day in May when we helped Etta onto the magic carpet that would whisk her off to her time warp in history. The kitchen had been provisioned with her dietary foods, her prettiest dresses were hanging in the closet, and Cleopatra never launched in more regal splendor as Etta took up her position in the recliner behind the copilot's seat with her afghan and a cup of jasmine tea.

Alice attended her mother; Dortha and I took over pilot and navigator duties. We phalanxed a parade of cars containing assorted relatives and spouses who wanted to be part of Etta's pilgrimage into the past. Our route was to take us over the towering Tetons, then down into Jackson Hole and across Wyoming to Torrington. We took our time, allowing our nostalgic passenger to soak up the beauty of the country she loved so well.

The journey to Wyoming was marred only by one incident: passing through the city of Twin Falls, Idaho, we were cruising down Main Street when suddenly a fire truck loomed up in my rearview mirror, horns blowing and lights flashing. I immediately pulled over to the right and stopped, giving the emergency vehicle the right of way. Unfortunately, the maneuver was quite abrupt.

This would have been no problem had not Etta elected this moment to start making her way to the rear of the coach to heed a nudge from nature. I suddenly found myself in downtown Twin Falls with an upended mother-in-law, pants at half-mast, who was telling me in no uncertain terms what she thought of my driving.

She was quickly mollified by her daughters, however, who were laughing so hard they could barely reseat their mother. Then my ill-advised acceleration after the fire truck passed heaped even further indignities upon the hapless woman, as there were now three women piled up in the john that barely accommodated one person.

I knew I would be forgiven by happy hour, however, as I was the only one who knew where the blackberry wine was stashed. I was.

As we roamed the remains of the homestead in which Etta had been raised, her eyes danced as she regaled us with the history of Rock Ranch at the turn of the century. It had been the mecca for the cattlemen who roamed the state, and she told of being bounced on the knees of the legendary Tom Horn, the gunslinger who had been hired to keep the sheepmen at bay. And her cheeks glowed as she told how the whole family would harness up the buckboard and travel all day to Fort Laramie so she and her sisters could spend the night dancing with the dashing young officers at the fort.

When our cortege returned to Boise a week later, Etta was genuinely sorry to leave the motorhome. Thanks to the marvels of RV technology and the love of a doting family, she had seen the realization of a lifelong dream come true.

Etta Power was now ready to shuffle off this mortal coil. Shortly after returning from our pilgrimage, she passed away peacefully in her sleep. As we laid her to rest, there was still a smile on her face and a hint of a blush on her cheeks.

The Civil War Buff

"You and your back roads!" said the missus, mopping up a dollop of coffee that had just divorced its cup. "You got something against nice, smooth freeways?"

"As you well know, my dove, all freeways look the same. It's the back-road country that tickles one's risibilities."

"Your risibilities may be tickling, but mine are vibrating. North Carolina has a lot of assets, but its back roads are not one of them."

"The Tar Heel State is, indeed, a thing of beauty." I suddenly realized more attention should have been paid to my driving and less to the redhead's mopping. Coming to a railroad track that crossed the road, I learned too late I was going too fast. An old, dilapidated camper we had been following hit the raised rails and literally flew across the tracks to land with an axle-bruising crunch on the other side.

By the time the sight had triggered poky reflexes, Rocinante was astraddle the tracks. Her front limbs went into a wild attack of the Saint Vitus dance, and all hell broke loose. "Gadzooks!" I yelled. "We've blown a tire. Maybe two!"

Limping stoically like a racehorse with a broken leg, Rocinante slowed down as I applied the brakes. Spotting a service station just ahead, I brought the wounded steed chattering into the station. I shut off the ignition and looked over at my white-faced sidekick as I dismounted. "Just pray that we don't have to shoot her."

"Oh, you poor baby!" said the wife, stroking the dash.

Down on all fours, I was pleasantly surprised to see there were no flat tires. Furthermore, the front-end shocks and stabilizers appeared normal. Completing my inspection, I was startled by a face that suddenly materialized beside the left wheel. "Bitch, ain't it!" said the face. I crawled out from under the rig to see a lean, elderly body was attached to the face. "Name's Jackson. That's my rig over there with the flat tire."

"I'm Anderson." I shook the proffered hand, while my eyes followed the finger pointing to the old camper that had hit the raised railroad tracks just ahead of us. "That railroad track!" I fumed. "I've traveled 6,000 miles in the boondocks on this trip without a problem. I hit this booby trap in North Carolina, and my front end starts shimmying like a go-go dancer."

"Know what you mean. I'm an ex-trucker, and I know a little bit about front ends. I'll take a look-see."

Before I could protest, he was on his back under Rocinante's forequarters. Ten minutes later he emerged, dusting himself off. "Looks okay to me. Nothing wrong with your front-end suspension far as I can tell. Could be your stabilizers. Sometimes if a wheel gets a bad jolt, it'll set up a chatter. The two shocks get to fighting each other. Makes a hellish shimmy."

"What do you do in a case like that?"

"Do what you did. Slow down. Let the equalizers get back in sync. You may need a new wheel alignment, but I don't see any structural damage."

"I'll try it out, but first let's check your rig."

"Already have. Didn't hurt my front end. Shocks and stabilizers are all shot anyway, so I just blew a tire. No sweat."

"I'll help you change it."

"No thanks. I'll tackle it after lunch." He looked around at the area. "So this is the state that lung cancer built."

"Just because North Carolina exports a lot of tobacco, I'm not sure the chamber of commerce would endorse your description."

"They ought to be ashamed of themselves," said Jackson, shaking a cigarette out of a pack. "Anything that burns holes in your shirts can't be very good for your lungs."

"Good point." I watched the old-timer light his cigarette. "You retired, Mr. Jackson?"

"Yep. You know the ol' story. I spent thirty years driving trucks and cussing out RVers so I could retire, buy an RV, and spend the rest of my life cussing out truckers."

"Makes sense. What do you do when you're not cussing out truck drivers?"

"I'm a Civil War buff. All my life I wanted to retire and follow the Civil War. Visit the battlefields. Relive the campaigns. Take Raleigh, for instance. It's a handsome city in the classic Southern tradition. Has a state capitol building that's over a century and a half old, and the restless bones of Andrew Jackson." He took a deep drag from his cigarette. "Don't you find that interesting?"

"Fascinating."

"I just spent a week in Petersburg, Virginia. Did you know that it was here Cornwallis gathered his British troops for the Yorktown Campaign? And a bloody trench war ensued that sapped Lee's Confederate Army and led to the fall of Richmond?"

"I'm afraid I'm a bit hazy on that. . . ."

"Parked for almost two months at Fredericksburg. Four great battlefields in that area. Chancellorsville, Fredericksburg, Spotsylvania Court House, and Wilderness. Many of the old landmarks have been preserved. James Monroe's law office, the house of George Washington's sister, the Rising Sun Tavern where patriots gathered. . . ."

"The Rising Sun Tavern? Now that might be worth seeing."

"Yep. I'm fulfilling my lifelong dream." He took a long drag from his cigarette, and then ground the butt out under his boot. "But I've bent your ear long enough. You'd better mount up and see if your front end's gonna wobble. If it does, bring it back and we'll work on it."

Thanking the man, I crawled behind the wheel. I cranked up and cautiously edged out onto the street. At slow speed there was no shimmy. I took a deep breath and accelerated. Still no shimmy.

At freeway speed Rocinante responded like the thoroughbred she is. It baffled me that her front end could hit a bad jolt, sending her into a horrible vibration that could shake fillings loose, and then settle down to a ride as smooth as goose grease. Like any lady of great propriety, she had taken exception at being sorely mistreated and had reacted with violent indignation. But then, having vented her spleen, she was quick to forgive when properly salved with a little TLC.

"That Mr. Jackson sure is a nice man," said the distaff, resuming her navigational duties. "I certainly envy him. I would love to spend a whole year reliving the history of the Civil War."

"I had a front-row seat for World War II. If you've seen one war, you've seen 'em all."

"No, sir. World War II didn't have Scarlett O'Hara and Rhett Butler."

"Might be fun at that. You explore the old battlefields, I'll explore the old taverns."

She gave me a grin. "I'll drink to that."

An Ode to
Valentine's Day

"Do you happen to know what day this is?" I looked across the cockpit at the distaff, who was batting her long lashes at me.

"Yes. Today's Friday. The day I flush out the black-water holding tank."

I was skewered on a look of disdain. "Today happens to be Saint Valentine's Day."

"Oh? Valentine's Day. And just what, my little cupid, would you deign to do to commemorate this most auspicious occasion? Besides helping me flush out the holding tank?"

"Very simple. I'd like to have a candlelit dinner at a very expensive restaurant."

"Ah, so. Your slightest wish is my command, mi amore." I checked my watch. "We're nearing Fort Stockton. I'll check the CB Yellow Pages for a suitable rotisserie." I flicked on the CB. "Breaker 19," I said, thumbing the transmitter. "Anyone reading Red Writer? Come back."

"Hi, y'all, Red Ryder," returned a clear voice that had been dipped in hominy grits. Since my wife is a redhead and I doodle with a typewriter, we had picked Red Writer as our CB handle. It always came back "Red Ryder." "Lonesome Polecat's mah handle. Eastbound. You're comin' in loud and clear. Must be close by."

I looked up the road to see a blue semi laboring up a long hill in front of us. "Lonesome Polecat, are you a blue 18-wheeler poking up a long hill?"

"That's a 10-4, good buddy. You the Dolphin motorhome comin' up on mah back porch?"

"That's a roger, Lonesome Polecat."

"Sorry to hold y'all up on this stretcha single-lane highway. Got an axle-bustin' load in this rig. But ah'll sho 'nuff give y'all the signal when the road's cleah up ahead."

"Many thanks, Lonesome Polecat. Don't sweat it. We're enjoying the scenery."

He let out a belly laugh. "Some scenery, ain't it? Partsa Texas would gag a maggot."

I pulled up behind the laboring truck. "Lonesome Polecat, you know anything about Fort Stockton? I'm looking for a good place to eat."

"Old Fort Stockton town? Afraid I can't help ya, good buddy. Ah've only passed through."

"No problem. I'll check REACT on my CB when we get there."

"Way to go." There was a pause, then, "Ah can see ovah the rise now, Red Ryder. Clear sailin.' Put the hammer down."

I slammed into overdrive and passed. Swinging back into the right lane, I transmitted my thanks.

"Mah pleasure, Red Ryder. Be seein' y'all soon. This rig don't bust no records goin' uphill, but it goes downhill like a roadrunner with a hotfoot."

Sure enough, five minutes later on a level stretch, the blue van gave a blast of air horns and smoked by us like a roadrunner with a hotfoot. "Have a good one, Red Ryder," was his parting remark as he thundered down the road.

I no sooner acknowledged than a sultry female voice came over the speaker. "Breaker 19, this is Frisky Fox. Do I hear the voice of a lonely trucker?"

I started reaching for the transmitter when I felt a slap on my wrist. I looked over at the wife. "You ain't no lonely trucker," she snapped.

"No. Of course not, dear." I retrieved my hand. "I'm a happily married man."

But it was apparent that Lonesome Polecat was not likewise fettered. "Hey there, Frisky Fox. Lonesome Polecat, heah. How y'all, little lady?"

"Jes as fine as frog hair, Lonesome Polecat. Which way you headin'?"

"Eastbound on good ole Eye-10. Aimin' to peel off at ole Fort Stockton town for a cuppa motion lotion."

"Well, ain't that a coincidence, Lonesome Polecat. I was jes thinkin' of doin' the same thing."

"How about that! Shore would be a pleasure, little lady, to buy y'all a cup of java."

"There's a truck stop on the edge of town, first one on the right-hand side. Meet you there. What's your rig?"

"Herdin' a blue Ford semi, little lady. Ah'll meet y'all there in about half an hour."

"That's a 10-4, Lonesome Polecat. Lookin' forward to it. I'm drivin' a cattle truck semi fulla live T-bones. Frisky Fox, out."

I looked over at the redhead. "Now isn't that sweet? Romance on the open road."

Dortha gave me the look. "You sure that's romance? Frisky Fox. Really!"

"Don't tell me, my pet, that romance has flown your soul. I think it's nice we have friendly people out there. Sort of Florence Nightingales of the Underpass, taking lonely truckers under their wings. They're probably with the chamber of commerce—sort of a Welcome Wagon."

"I'll bet the Frisky Fox does some welcome waggin', all right."

"Dortha Anderson! Are you suggesting there might be a commercial connotation to the expressions of friendship we have just been privy to?"

"The thought's crossed my mind."

"Shame on you!"

Thirty minutes later we hit the Fort Stockton city limits. I slowed up, watching for the first truck stop on the right-hand side. Sure enough, looming up ahead was the blue van parked at the side of the station. There was a cattle truck parked beside it. A young, Stetsoned trucker was helping a slender woman down from her cab. Taking her arm, he escorted her toward the diner.

"See there!" I said in triumph. "He's only buying her a cup of coffee."

"So it appears. I'm glad."

"Yep, due to the marvel of electronics, the Lonesome Polecat is no longer lonesome, and the Frisky Fox is frisking. Isn't that beautiful?"

Dortha sighed. "We live in a crazy world. We used to go to a barn dance or a church social to meet people. Now the thing to do is get a cattle truck and a CB."

"You've come a long way, baby. Still think that the Frisky Fox is soliciting?"

"No. But I know the CB is being used for that purpose. I've heard it."

I looked at her. "Wife, are you forgetting this is Valentine's Day? There are times when I think you are becoming a real cynic."

"Oh? A cynic, am I? Well, let me tell you something, Bunky.

I catch you getting mixed up with any of these pavement princesses, and I'll tie a knot in your CB antenna. An' that's a 10-fo', fo' sho, fo' sho."

Ah, the lure of the open road. There's just something romantic about spending Saint Valentine's Day in the bosom of our fantastic, free-wheeling fraternity of the beckoning back roads—especially if one is married to a redhead.

The Infernal Revenue Service

Led into one of the cubicle offices of the Internal Revenue Service, I looked at the comely young lady who had risen from her desk to greet me.

"Glad to meet you, Mr. Anderson," she said, extending her hand.

"And I you, Mrs. Hastings." I shook her hand. "You don't look like a vampire," I said wittily.

"Contrary to popular opinion, all IRS auditors do not suck blood, shy from garlic, or turn into bats. Please have a seat, sir." I took the proffered chair in front of her desk. "So you're a writer."

"I say I am. My editors and book reviewers often don't agree with me."

"I've never audited a writer before. I do hope you'll bear with me."

"I've never had a full audit before. We'll just tiptoe through the mine fields hand in hand."

She gave me an odd look as she opened a voluminous file. "First, I have no problem with you deducting your office-in-home expense. You have established yourself as a professional writer. In fact, I've even read one of your books. Something called *Taming Mighty Alaska in an RV.*"

I grinned expansively. "Splendid. Did you like it?"

"No."

My grin evaporated. "Sorry about that."

"But my husband did. He has absolutely no taste in literature."

"May we move right along, Mrs. Hastings?"

"Yes. As I told you in my letter, there are three items on your 1996 tax return that require an explanation. First, the barbells." She flipped through her file. "Here it is. You claim a deduction of $65 for a set of barbells you donated to the Salvation Army."

"That is true."

"How much did you pay for the barbells?"

"Sixty-five dollars."

"How long did you have them?"

"Approximately ten years."

She gave me a wry smile. "You did not take depreciation into account when you made your deduction."

"Depreciation?" I looked at her askance. "How in blazes can barbells depreciate? They're made of cast-iron. Bought them for my son. Only times they were ever lifted was when my wife dusted under the bed."

"Nevertheless, we must figure in some sort of a depreciation table. . . ."

"No, we mustn't. Not on barbells. If they had been found in King Tut's tomb, they'd still be good as new. If anything, they've appreciated over the years."

"Well," she said as she puckered her brows, "I'll take what you say under advisement." She checked her notes. "Next item: You did deduct a depreciation on your motorhome. Would you care to explain that?"

"Happy to. Motorhomes do depreciate. And since I use my motorhome in my business. . . ."

"Just how do you justify that, sir?"

"Simple. I have published three books on RVing and numerous magazine articles. I do a monthly column for the Cadillac of the RVing magazines, *MotorHome*. Naturally, I have to have a motorhome to do my research."

She mulled this. "Research?"

"Of course. I can't write about RVing if I don't get out and RV—do my homework. The Infernal Revenooers never question the goodly amount of taxes I pay on book royalties. They must not question the expenses required in producing that income."

"I see." She studied me out of the corner of her eye as she chewed this. "I'll make a note of that." She turned to her file. "One last item: entertainment expense."

"Lay it on me."

"You have listed one item of $247 for hotel-room renovation. Would you care to explain how that would be entertainment expense?"

"Certainly. I had to buy new drapes and wallpaper for a room in the Holiday Inn when I was entertaining a guest."

"I don't follow."

"Well, we were having this pre-wedding stag party for a bachelor, when the topless dancer jumped out of the cake. Somehow, one of the cake's candles caught the drapes on fire."

I tried to smile disarmingly.

"And just how did you justify this as entertainment expense?"

"Well, you have to admit it was entertaining, and it did turn out to be an expense. The bachelor we were honoring was the editor of one of my books. Just before the dancer jumped out of the cake, we were talking about the revisions of my latest tome."

"I am afraid this one isn't going to wash, Mr. Anderson."

"Admittedly, it is a gray area."

"Gray area? Donkey hockey is what it is."

I studied my fingernails. "I don't feel as strongly about this as I do about the barbells and the motorhome. But you must admit that gray areas are open to interpretation. I think my interpretations are just as valid as those of the IRS."

She smiled sweetly. "We'll just have to see about that." She closed the file. "I have no more questions. Do you, Mr. Anderson?"

"No."

"I thank you very much for your time and cooperation. You will hear shortly of the IRS' decisions concerning your audit." She held out her hand. "Nice meeting you, sir."

"Likewise, I'm sure."

A month later, the results were in. I had won two, lost one. The barbells were allowed, the entertainment expense was denied. However, the IRS had used a different accelerating table for the depreciation on our motorhome, and the final audit showed the IRS owed us a nice hunk of change. A check, plus interest, arrived the next day.

So, fellow taxpayers, from this experience several lessons may be drawn:

1. Keep meticulously honest records when filing your income tax. I was able to account for every postage stamp I deducted, which started me off on the right foot.

2. If treated civilly, IRS people respond in like fashion. Walking in with a flame thrower or a grenade belt has a tendency to start the meeting off in the wrong direction.

3. Do not be intimidated by the IRS logo, and do not hesitate to fight for your rights. Gray areas are settled in the taxpayer's favor as often as they are in the IRS's favor.

And lastly, if you're in the market for a set of ten-year-old barbells in mint condition, just drop me a line. I know where there's one whale of a buy.

How to Survive a
Family Reunion

It ranks right up there in popularity with an Internal Revenue Service audit and a root canal. I refer, of course, to the family reunion.

Psychologists can probably tell us what kind of gene mutation we all have that makes a clan want to occasionally flock together and clutch one another like a family of baboons being threatened by a stalking hyena. Happily, this rite of spring seldom happens more than once a year, and, if carefully watched and controlled, the familiar bonding may be prevented from getting completely out of hand.

Big Red and I have prided ourselves on keeping family reunions to a minimum. In fact, by resorting to subterfuge and chicanery, we have been able to stall off get-togethers for nearly ten years. But, alas, our good fortune was not destined to last forever. Last year, bowing to pressures from both our families, we were euchred into holding a family get-together.

Looking back on the mayhem, however, things could have been much worse. We had to cancel the watermelon-seed spitting contest because Uncle Bus couldn't find his teeth, and the family home movies had to be canceled because they got mixed up with Cousin Spike's collection of porno flicks—which really made inroads on the popcorn before we realized the mistake.

But the main reason we cut our losses to a minimum was because we capitalized on past experiences. I would like to share some of these with you because—like it or not—sooner or later you're going to get hooked into attending and/or planning a family reunion. When that happens, the following tips and anecdotes just might help steer you around the rocky shoals of calamitous clan conventions.

Timing is, of course, paramount. Reunions should always be planned during warm weather, as this will help keep the ankle-biters and Pamper-puddlers outside of the house as much as possible. If someone's home must be used, a large backyard is recommended for big gatherings, so the children can eat outdoors with the dog.

To further discuss location, never—but never—have the family reunion at your house. Not only did we not have this recent reunion at our home, we didn't even hold it in our town. Instead, our planning committee wisely decided to hold it in a neutral zone, in the middle of the state.

Consequently, some thirty-eight assorted clan members met in a little town called Stanley, Idaho. Here the Middle Fork of the Salmon River provides great white-water rafting, and the Sawtooth Mountains are so rugged they can even weather a family foofaraw. The reunion dinner was a smashing success—barely marred by the baby moose that was smuggled into the dining room by the younger set. And after a day of rafting, the troops were so tired, they barely managed to wreck one dance hall before retiring.

The following day, we moseyed over the scenic Galena Pass and into Sun Valley, Idaho. Months before, we had nailed down tickets for the ice-skating show that featured Kristi Yamaguchi, the cute little whipstitch who won the gold medal in the Olympics figure-skating competition. If you must have a reunion, remember to keep clansmen busy with all sorts of interesting activities—preferably in the next state.

Now we come to a most important facet of your upcoming confab. It is essential that you go armed with a few choice reunion bromides with which to impress your relatives. As a public service, the following quotes overheard at our last reunion may be used. Some of these have a few whiskers, but they are all apropos.

For instance, to quote Aunt Alice: "Successful reunions are all due to successful planning. I always eat lots of garlic before attending. That way, people can't get close enough to see my wrinkles."

Says Uncle Fred, who is two years older than dirt: "I may not have graduated in the top half of my class, but I was in the group that made the top half possible."

Cousins Emily and Don, who were awarded the prize for being the couple who had been married the longest, set the record straight. Says Em, "Don and I haven't really been married the longest. It just seems that way. And we're getting so old that Don's idea of a little action is discovering his prune juice is working."

Aunt Charlotte, an attractive Swede, cut right to the chase: "If you can't attend a reunion looking skinny, go looking rich."

And nephew Kip came up with: "I don't know why I keep coming to reunions. Most of the guys are so fat and bald-headed, they don't even recognize me."

Says Uncle Joe, "I thought everyone else at the reunion looked old, until I stopped to help that little, old, gray-haired lady across the street. Turned out to be my wife."

To really put the cap on the old-poop bromides, it was Aunt Melva who said, "Bus and I have found the perfect method of birth control at our age. It's called nudity."

But it was son Scott who really nailed the reunion syndrome: "An amazing thing happens at reunions. People actually get all choked up and nostalgic about things they weren't all that crazy about the first time around."

Of course, the most ideal place to hold a reunion is at a nice RV park. If everyone owns or rents an RV, great reunions can be planned that take in several venues. Also, by having your own metal cocoon, you may climb into it anytime the revelry gets out of hand. And there is nothing more enjoyable than getting the wagons in a circle and having a good old bonfired, clod-stompin' hoedown.

You are now properly equipped for planning and/or being the life of the party at your next reunion. Like having a hemorrhoidectomy, this rendezvous must be met with fortitude, true grit, and an open mind. With the proper attitude, reunions may not only be painless, but may provide a modicum of enjoyment—particularly if they are held in somebody else's hometown.

The Christmas Present

One would not normally opt to spend Christmas in a western Kansas prairie smack in the middle of nowhere. However, in a freak accident, a pheasant had tried to mate with Rocinante's windshield at a closing speed of about Mach 1, and before Dortha knew it, she had received her first serving of pheasant under glass. So instead of heading east for a jubilant Yuletide get-together with family and friends, we found ourselves stranded in the remote vicinage of Oakley, Kansas, awaiting the shipment of a windshield replacement.

Everyone in Kansas must go to the Bahamas in December, as there are no RV parks open. After spotting several rigs parked in a trailer court, we checked it out and found we could park there if we didn't need any hookups other than electrical. We lost no time reining our battered beast into the trailer court and putting on her oat bag.

Always making the best of a situation, Dortha decided that since it looked like we would not be near the ones we loved at Christmas, we should love the ones we were near. In no time at all my roommate had launched into lifetime friendships with the RVers on each side of us.

We admired a chilly kaleidoscopic Kansas sunset with a couple of vagabonds in their eighties who hailed from Wisconsin, and a widower from Nevada who was traveling in a small Ford camper with four dogs, three cats, and a very nervous parakeet.

"There are times," said the Nevadan, "when I even wish I had my wife back."

But we both fell in love with the chipper octogenarians who were celebrating the occasion of just turning 100,000 miles on the odometer of their Southwind.

"We don't need much of an excuse to bust out the lemonade," giggled Maggie Simpson, a lively little sparrow. "Of course Homer always adds a dash of sour mash to his when no one's looking."

"That's a lot of miles on a motorhome," I said, admiring the well-maintained rig.

Maggie pooh-poohs the thought with a wave of her hand. "Pshaw, it's nothing. This is our second roving home. Would you believe that we ran the wheels right off a Holiday trailer before we traded up to this motorhome?"

"Really?" asked Dortha.

"That's right," said Homer. "Had a couple hundred thousand miles on her when we traded her in. You might say we sorta pioneered this way of life."

"It all started," said Maggie, "when I retired from my teaching job and Homer retired from the railroad. Well, we found out you can only do so much rockin' on the front porch without going batty. So we decided there must be more to life than just rockin' into the hereafter. That's when we got the idea. Sold the house, and we've been roaming ever since."

I studied the faces of the travelers. The march of time had left footprints on their features, but their eyes were clear and sharp and their faculties unimpaired. "I would say this way of life has certainly agreed with you both."

Homer added, "Hell's bells, we've never felt better. You know what causes senility and old age? It ain't the clock. It's boredom. Rust. We just don't have time to get bored." He pointed to his coach. "If it weren't for old Betsy here, we'd been angleworm chow a long time ago."

"Land sakes, I guess," said Maggie. "Nobody enjoys life more than we do. We have a bushel of grandkids scattered around the country that we have to keep tabs on. And Homer likes to fish. If he finds a good hole, we're likely to take root in one place a week. I'm a rock hound, so while he's fishing I'm hunting for rocks."

"That's marvelous," said Dortha.

"Yep," added Homer, "Betsy's paid for. We eat a lot of fish I catch. We go out into the fields and pick fruit and vegetables during season and Maggie cans 'em. We each get a little retirement pay from our jobs, and along with Social Security we don't even have to dip into our nest egg. Fact is, we even save a little each month for our old age. We can spit in anybody's eye."

"Homer!" said Maggie, giving her spouse a dirty look. "That is a terribly uncouth expression."

Homer beamed at us over his bourbon-laced lemonade. "Never said I was couth, Maggie."

"But being a schoolteacher most of my life," said Maggie, "what I like best is getting out and seeing all the places I've been teaching about for so many years. The Grand Canyon, Niagara Falls, New England when the leaves turn gold—shucks, we not only saw the Florida Everglades, we lived in them for three months. How marvelous it is to see a dusty old geography book come to life!"

Dortha nodded. "I would say you folks have found your Shangri-la."

"And," added Maggie, her eyes twinkling, "our Arcadia, Goshen, and Agapemone all wrapped into one and put on rolling wheels."

Homer gave his wife a puzzled look. "Fella should think

twice about marryin' a schoolteacher. Half the time I don't know what the Hades she's talkin' about."

"I have a feeling," I said, grinning at Homer, "that your wife is happy with Betsy." I looked at Maggie. "The only reservation my wife has about fulltiming it is not having plants and flowers. The redhead has an acute case of green-thumbitis."

"Heavens to mercy," said Maggie, "what woman hasn't? Let's step into the house a minute. I'll show you how we handle this problem."

Approaching the coach, we noticed the window boxes on the outside laden with snapdragons, carnations, and sweet peas. Entering the motorhome was like walking into a greenhouse. There were plants in pots, plants in planters, plants in macramé hangers—in every nook and cranny. A sweet-potato vine framed the galley window; a creeping Charley crept out of an elegant copper cuspidor-turned-planter to make green-fingered advances on the living-room rocking chair. Dortha went into a catatonic rapture as the two women lost themselves completely in the nether world of botany.

We put up only token resistance when invited over for Christmas dinner the following day. The dinner was everything an old-fashioned repast should be, complete with Christmas presents under the tiny, live tree that commanded the front room.

We emerged from the Simpson hothouse laden with loot; Dortha with her arms full of plant cuttings, I with half a wild-rhubarb pie under my arm and a handful of polished agates. As we expressed our gratitude, Maggie asked us if we'd like to go exploring with them in the morning.

"What is there to explore around here?" I asked.

"Lots," said Maggie. "We may stay several days."

"In Oakley, Kansas? There's nothing for a billion miles but wheat fields! And they're all frozen."

"Thousands of people whiz right by here on the freeway thinking the same thing, not so much as giving this little town a thought. But do you know that just a few miles south of here are the Pyramid Rocks? Marvelous old eroded chalk pinnacles that contain reptilian fossils from an age when the earth's crust was still forming?"

"I must confess I did not."

She shook her finger at me. "So there you are, young man. That's the trouble with people today. Everyone's in such a hurry! We build bigger and faster freeways and cars so people can get places faster—to do what? People race through life like the 'fast forward' button on their VCR. Stop to smell the flowers? They don't even know what a flower looks like. Now you folks take the advice of two old poops who've been around. Just try moseying along the back roads sometimes. Enjoy the scenery. It will give you a new lease on life."

We missed the Christmas hustle and bustle with our friends and relatives that year. In fact, we barely got home by New Year's. For you see, we had taken to heart one of the finest Christmas presents we had ever been given.

It was very difficult to really see the Pyramid Rocks with their old chalk pinnacles containing fossils from an age when the crust was still forming.

It took us several days.

The Cop with the
Bedroom Eyes

Historic Savannah, Georgia, is one of the first planned cities in North America. And it's a charmer. Resplendent with broad avenues, cobblestoned riverfront, and squares shaded by majestic trees, Savannah is a beautiful city in spite of being designed by a couple of military types named General Oglethorpe and Colonel Bull.

We did all the neat touristy things, soaking up the culture of this great southern city as we moseyed around in Rocinante. Come lunchtime, we were ready for a hearty repast. "How would you, my dove," I asked my favorite wife, "like to eat at one of Savannah's most noted restaurants?"

"I'd love it," said Dortha. "Lead on, McDuff."

I drove into the parking lot of the Pirate's House, an eaterie renowned for its fine cuisine and historic charm. Finding ample room in the far end of the parking lot, I reined up Rocinante, hobbled her, and prepared for lunch. Dortha went to the fridge, slapped together some sandwiches, and uncorked a couple of colas. Then we hiked up our feet and had lunch while watching the long line of people waiting to get into the restaurant.

"Never let it be said," said the spouse, "that you don't know how to show a lady a good time. We eat in the parking lots of some of the world's finest restaurants."

"Nothing's too good for my true love," said I, bestowing upon her my most beguiling grin. "Pass the potato chips."

After several days enjoying this marvelous city, it was time to slap Rocinante on the flanks and head north. We soon crossed the Eugene Talmadge Memorial Bridge and were in South Carolina. Northbound Interstate 95 undulates in gentle fashion through the Palmetto State's rolling woodlands and farms, sideswiping such intriguing towns as Coosawhatchie, Pocataligo, and Yemassee.

We cruised along blissfully, monitoring the truckers' frequency on the CB, enjoying the chatter and the drawl of the knights of the road. Approaching Lake Marion, the radio suddenly crackled with a voice dipped in hominy grits. "Double nickel! Double nickel! Roadblock at the junction of 26 and I-95. Whole den of Smokeys. Double nickel!"

Seldom did this warning strike terror into our hearts, as speeding was never a worry. Rocinante had developed a touch of consumption, so we just put her cruise control on fifty-five, got in the right lane, and watched the world go by. It was embarrassing to be passed by funeral processions and old glaciers, but we like to smell the roses while traveling.

As predicted, several patrol cars at the intersection were stopping traffic coming from both directions. I braked as a patrolman approached the driver's window.

"Gee," said Dortha. "He's cute."

"There's no such thing," I replied, "as a cute policeman."

"Sorry to trouble you, folks," said the officer, returning Dortha's smile. "We're checking all traffic for an escaped convict."

"I don't think we have any escaped convicts, officer," I said, turning to the spouse. "Do we, dear?"

"I don't think so. I cleaned the coach good this morning. Didn't run across any."

"How about the john?" I asked her. "Do you want to check, in case he crawled in during our last rest stop?"

"If he crawled in during our last rest stop, you check the john."

"Very well, dear." I did as directed, returning with a negative report. "Sorry, officer, we seem to be fresh out of escaped convicts."

"Thank you, sir. I apologize for the inconvenience."

"It's our pleasure," said the missus, batting cow eyes at the lawman.

"By the way, officer," I said, buckling back in. "What do you patrolmen think of the truckers yakking back and forth on their CBs, warning one another when your patrol cars are sighted?"

The officer grinned. "It's great."

I looked at him in surprise. "It's great?"

"Really. We monitor their conversations. Sometimes we even give warnings ourselves. We figure our presence is then known over maybe a twenty- to thirty-mile stretch of highway, because the truckers relay the information. Broadens our deterrence. If this gets them to slow down to legal speed, that's what our job's all about."

"I never looked at it that way," I remarked.

"We had a dangerous stretch of highway called Suicide Hill. Truckers tried to take it too fast. We parked an old police car nearby, put a dummy dressed in a uniform in it, and we haven't had an accident since. Thanks to CB, truckers slow down twenty miles before hitting Suicide Hill. Saves lives. We're all for truckers yakking their heads off on their chatterboxes."

"Fascinating."

"You heading very far north?"

"To Washington, D.C."

"Then beware of some of those northern states. The patrolmen are coming up with some pretty fancy tricks. They soup up a hay truck, then get on their CB and advise there isn't a Smokey for miles in any direction. The truckers put their hammers down, then the officers swoop in for the kill. They don't expect to be arrested by a farmer driving a hay truck. Next day the police might use an egg truck. Maybe a semi. Once they even used a hearse."

"That," I said, "is really hitting below the belt. Being arrested by a hearse driver."

The officer grinned. "Just goes to show you can't trust those damn Yankees." He gave a two-fingered salute. "You all take it easy up there. And have a good day."

"Same to you," said Dortha. As we passed through the cordon and picked up speed, the wife turned to me. "What a nice man! Did you notice his eyes?"

"They looked beady."

"They did not! They looked beautiful. Bedroom eyes. And those lashes. They could shade South Carolina."

"I've never gotten into the habit of noticing cops' eyelashes. But I admit he did have a nice personality. Funny thing about the South. According to TV movies, southern cops all have personalities like speed bumps. Gorilla rejects. The one we just met could charm the teeth off a buzzsaw. So much for Hollywood stereotypes."

"I just don't understand," said Dortha, sighing, "how it ever happened."

"How what ever happened?"

"The Civil War."

"Not sure I follow."

"With eyelashes like that, how did the Southerners ever lose the war?"

I knew better than to touch that logic. I looked over at my pretty wife. "I'm not so sure the South lost the war."

A Lion in Winter

El Paso, Texas, is probably not a place you would fly to from Hawaii or Bermuda to spend your honeymoon. But if you take the trouble to scratch around a little, you may uncover several redeeming things about this bustling border town.

Big Red and I had spent a busy day doing just that and come happy hour had plugged into a local campground and put the nose bag on Rocinante. Hitting the sack early, I was blissfully sawing wood when suddenly my reverie was punctured by a sharp elbow in the ribs. "Honey!" said the distaff. "Wake up."

I managed to prop one eyelid open. "Whuzza matter?"

"I just heard the most god-awful noise."

"Sorry. I'll try not to snore."

"Not your snoring. I swear it sounded like a lion."

I pried the other eyelid open. "You heard a lion?"

"Several lions. Roaring to each other."

"You mean lions? With manes and tails and lots of teeth? Like in *Born Free*?"

"That kind of lion."

"Probably the geese."

"It's not the geese."

"Squirrels in heat sometimes make noises like . . ."

"I know a lion when I hear one. Sounded like they were right outside."

"You had too many enchiladas for dinner. They don't allow lions running around loose, even in Texas." I listened for a moment. "See? It's nothing. Now go back to sleep."

"I know I heard a lion."

"I'm cutting off your *Wild Kingdom* on the boob tube before bedtime. Now go to sleep."

"Sorry I woke you up."

"So am I."

She rolled over. "I know I heard lions."

I started to chide the wife at breakfast the next morning about hearing lions roaring in the night. "I heard lions!" she snapped. Noting the danger signals lurking behind green eyes, I didn't press the subject. Instead I polished off the last pancake and went out to wash the rig.

I was up on Rocinante's roof with my long-handled scrub brush when Dortha came bounding out the door. She yelled up at me. "Andy, I've got a problem."

I crawled out of my bucket. "I've got a few solutions. Maybe one will fit."

"The oven isn't working. And I have a cake in it."

"You've come to the right man." I shinnied down from the roof and tackled the Coleman oven. Twenty minutes later I found that only one of my solutions worked: call a Coleman repairman. "I think it's the safety valve. The regulator isn't kicking on when the thermocouple is heated. We'll have to have it looked at."

"Okay," said the wife. "But in the meantime I've got two pans full of cake dough. They'll be ruined."

"I'll get on the horn and see if we can get a Coleman man out here pronto."

As I started out the door, I almost bumped into a man wearing a kimono and a cowboy hat. Obviously he was just returning from the shower, as he had a towel over his shoulder and the white hair under his hat was wet. I apologized for almost bowling him over.

He brushed aside my apology, saying, "Didja get your oven fixed?"

I gave him a blank look. I was used to the great camaraderie and close-knit ties of the RV fraternity but was at a loss as to how a person in the shower could be privy to our problems in the motorhome. "Not yet," I said.

"Couldn't help hearin' ya on my way to the shower. Hard not to hear when yer shoutin' from the top a yer rig."

"Guess it is at that. I'm going to the phone to get a repairman out here."

"What about yer batter?"

"It's going to have to wait."

"Spoil."

I shrugged. "Not much I can do about it at the moment. What kind of pancakes does cake dough make?"

"Lemme have it. I'll bake it." He jerked his thumb toward a disheveled motorhome parked nearby "That's ma rig. Ain't no fancy lashup lak you got here, but the dang stove works."

"Well, now that's what I call real neighborly."

"Git it."

I summoned Dortha to the door and outlined the neighbor's offer. She was delighted. As she gathered up the cake pans I asked the elderly gentleman, "Where you from?"

"Earth," he said.

"Earth, eh?" I gave him a sidelong glance. "That's nice. I'd hate to think our devil's food cake is being baked by someone from another planet."

He gave me an odd look. "Hey, I'm from Earth, Texas."

"Aha! Of course. Earth, Texas."

"Up inna panhandle. Near Muleshoe and Circle Back."

"Of course. That Earth, Texas. What do you do up there, pardner?"

Dortha came to the door with the two pans. The old Texan took one and I took the other. "I'll show you what I do after I get these cakes inna oven." I gave the wife a look of helplessness, then followed the flapping kimono toward the ancient motorhome in the distance.

An hour later I was back with the baked cake layers. Dortha stuck a toothpick in one, pulled it out, and examined it, looking pleased. "Beautiful."

"I know. It's already been tested. The nice old gent tested it with a broom straw."

Dortha looked pained. "Not a dirty broom straw."

"No way. He sanitized it with tobacco juice."

"Thank goodness." She started removing the cake from the tins. "Nice man. What does he do for a living?"

"You don't really want to know."

"If I didn't want to know, I wouldn't have asked."

"OK. He takes care of pussycats. I gotta go call the Coleman people."

"Pussycats? He takes care of pussycats?"

"Large pussycats. Got any change for the phone?"

"Large pussycats. Like maybe lions?"

"Like maybe lions. I gotta go."

"Lions! Aha!"

I tried to ignore the spatula of chocolate frosting waving in my face. "Seems there's half a dozen lions in a huge truck that's parked over by the office."

"Oo-ha!"

"Part of a rodeo act. Had to pull in here last night to wait out the blizzard up north. Sam's the roustabout. Feeds 'em, cleans the cages. . . ."

"So! I hear lions roaring in the night, and you're ready to ship me off to the rubber room."

I wiped the frosting off the end of my nose. "Honey, you have to admit that being yanked from a deep sleep with the news that we're surrounded by lions is a bit . . ."

"From now on, when I tell you I hear lions roaring in the night, I want no smart chatter from you."

"Yes, dear. You may hear roaring lions, snapping turtles, or braying hyenas, and I will believe you. Now may I go call the Coleman people?"

She gave me a scalding look of triumph. "You may. Out!"

Sometimes women can truly be a sand trap in the putting green of life.

Snoring Is Never Boring

There are many reasons why we mobile mavens enjoy the RVing lifestyle: the grandeur of the great outdoors, the joy of meeting interesting people from all walks of life, the enhancement of one's cerebral capacity by seeing the odd and wondrous places of the world.

And, of course, there's the fine art of snoring.

H. Allen Smith, a humorist of the old school, once made a collection of the sounds of toilet flushes. In his rovings around the world, he was always accompanied by his tape recorder. With one hand energizing the recorder, the other hand on the chain, he yanked for posterity the soothing sounds of cascading water in exotic porcelain furniture ranging from Maine to Mozambique. His favorite was a recording of the toilet flush in the men's room on the Orient Express, which was melodiously punctuated by the clickety-clack of steel rails.

Although not into such scatological pursuits myself, I must confess that I have a thing for snoring. I find that one's nocturnal exhalations can be utterly fascinating. A confessed closet snortopheliac (one who digs the snorings of other people), I found myself so intrigued by the subject that I now have quite an extensive collection of other peoples' snorts, rasps, rales, and heavy breathing.

For the pure snortopheliac, there is no better way to savor the expirations of our fellow man (and woman) than by the use of our roaming residence, especially when hooked up in crowded urban campgrounds. Due to the close proximity of neighbors, on a nice summer evening with the windows open, nasal nocturnes also sneak in with the breeze, bringing joy to the hearts of the most jaded snore-lover.

When hooking up in a full Dawson City RV park one evening, we were sandwiched in so close to our neighbors that we had to take turns opening the doors of our rigs. On this summer evening, I was able to count the night music coming from no less than five different directions. Truly a night to remember. And there was that summer night in Saskatchewan, when my loving spouse elbowed my ribs black and blue trying to get me to turn over, when the stentorian wheezings were actually coming from the Winnebago three spaces away.

As any purist will tell you, there are many different varieties of snorers. For the sake of brevity, we will discuss just a few of the more familiar ones. See if your mate falls into one of these categories:

The Snort and Whistle. This is the snorer who draws in breath with a snort, then exhales slowly through pursed lips to make a whistling sound. It is rumored that George Washington was of this species, and the wind breezing through his wooden teeth gave a very melodic flute sound. Although beautiful to hear, this type is not without its shortcomings. A gentleman in Montpelier, Idaho, woke up one morning to find his siren song had summoned five dogs, a dozen chipmunks, and a large moose with a bad head cold.

The Fluttering Lips. This somewhat rare species is identified by the sputtering noises that come from loose lips. This type, unfortunately, is seldom invited on fishing expeditions. The fluttering sound keeps fellow campers awake all night, as they keep thinking someone is trying to steal their outboard motorboat.

The Lullaby. This snorer is always welcome at slumber parties. This species is found in people with very shallow breathing and is punctuated occasionally by a soft snort to take in needed oxygen. It is fortunate that the soft snorts appear, as this is the only indication that the Lullaby snorer has, indeed, not gone off to the great campground in the sky.

The Addled Adenoids. This unfortunate snorer seems to get the most flak. But it's only because people don't take the trouble to really get to know a member of the AA. This is the person with a deviated sump pump who can truly deliver a rafter-rattling exhalation. We once encountered an AA member in Hays, Kansas, whose exhilarating exhausts not only registered on the Richter Scale, but managed to shatter the glass in the door of our microwave oven. You can always tell a member of the AA species, as the spouse wears earmuffs to bed.

The Cream-Fed Kitten. This is one who snores with almost a purring sound. I'm happy to report that my wife, Big Red, is a member of this group. The nasal tones resemble a purring kitten that has just polished off a bowl of whipped cream. The only drawback is that the Cream-Fed-Kitten-snorer types keep wanting to lick their spouse's face.

The Choo-Choo Train. This sleeper issues little puffs of air, not unlike The Little Train That Could. More than one delightful evening has been spent at a chili feed with the Throckmortons from Missoula, Montana. The husband always took a nap after dinner, and we would make bets as to how long Jeremiah could keep aloft a feather that had been placed on his nose.

The Buzzsaw. This is one of the most common species of the nocturnal noisemaker. Like the Addled Adenoids, when running at full throttle, this snorer has been known to add another crack in the San Andreas fault line. It is easy to distinguish this species, as people for miles around keep yelling "Timber!"

Thus we have the most prevalent of the broad categories of carefree cacophony. Many people enjoy derivations, or combinations of these categories, resulting in a host of subspecies too numerous to mention. This litany applies, of course, only to those who retire at night. Daytime sleepers, and those who are married to snoring vampires, have an entirely different set of circumstances, which will have to be covered in a future book.

Ornithologists have a bird book, in which they make notations on the various birds they encounter. Now that nearly everyone has a tape recorder, snortopheliacs can record for the ages the different fascinating respirations that permeate the night.

We RVers are truly blessed. For the true, genuine snortopheliac, there is no better environment in the world to record the various snoring species than in the marvelous, wheezing, snorting, palpitant world of the crowded RV campground.

So, be the first one in your campsite to start your own fascinating collection of stentorian exhausts. As a new hobby, it could well replace bird-watching, stamp collecting, and nude-beach bathing.

Snoring is never boring, and it beats the heck out of recording toilet flushes.

Good Nudists
Leave No Stern Untanned

One of the greatest perks of writing a column is the interesting mail that comes from folks cruising this great land in their migratory mansions.

Case in point is an intriguing letter that came from a charming couple who reside in Southbridge, Massachusetts. The communique concludes with: "I do not know if you or your wife and Rocinante have ever visited a clothes-optional RV park or not. I do, however, recommend it to you. I am sure Rocinante would appreciate not having her shades drawn." The letter was signed, "Yours in the sun."

Big Red and I have galloped Rocinante across the length and breadth of our homeland, but in all our travels have never encountered a clothes-optional RV park. It grieves me to confess this ignorance, but I didn't even know such a thing existed. Needless to say, I lost little time in contacting "Yours in the sun" for more information.

Further information was quickly provided. I suddenly found myself the recipient of a handsome, full-color publication titled *North American Guide to Nude Recreation*. In addition to showing lots of pictures of people who like to run around barefoot up to their dewlaps, it lists nude recreational areas in most states of the union and many provinces in Canada. And,

I'm happy to report, many of the landed clubs contain full RV hookups and amenities.

If the photos are to be believed, everyone seems to be having a great time indulging in all manner of activities, completely oblivious to holes in the ozone layer. A sense of humor seems to dominate the nudists as they slug their clubs with such names as Bares-N-Cubs, Free Spirits, Full-Tan Sun Club, Solar Bears, Garden of Eden, Rawhide Ranch, Tanfastics, and Bare-B-Ques.

Now, how does one go about checking into an RV park where one may play volleyball wearing nothing but a large grin? It's easy. Drop a line to the American Association for Nude Recreation (AANR), 1703 N. Main Street, Suite E, Kissimmee, Florida 34744-3396. They will send you a packet of goodies, including a list of clubs, the AANR philosophy, and an enrollment form. For a modest charge, you and your mate may become properly certified nudists, which entitles you to make your reservations at one of the many RV facilities listed in their recreation guide.

Not to be outdone, the AANR even offers a line of products for sale, including a raft of nudist books, gold pendants with the AANR logo, and—oddly enough—T-shirts. The latter, however, are tastefully lettered with these words: I'M COMPLETELY NUDE UNDER MY CLOTHES!

Also enclosed is a handbook that answers most of your questions, such as "My figure is less than Greek. Will I feel out of place?" Answer: "No. About one figure in twenty at a nudist park will be exemplary." And judging by the nudists depicted in the "Guide to Nude Recreation," this should be underscored. Dyed-in-the wool bare buffers seem to have a penchant for meat and potatoes, which has produced some torsos so large they shouldn't back up without a beeper.

Further research discloses that even the most bombastic nature-lover, however, feels it is prudent to don raiments when conducting certain chores. According to one nudist interviewed, prudence dictates that some types of coverage should be worn when frying bacon, and well-endowed women should consider wearing a halter when pounding poi.

In spite of its many attractions, I'm afraid airing one's privates in public is not in the cards for the frau and myself. Dortha is so modest she still wears her bathing suit with the holes in the knees while taking a shower, and I have bought surgeons so many Porsches that my manly torso looks like an aerial map of Bangladesh. So for the Andersons, the days of skinny-dipping are probably behind us.

In all honesty, the AANR does seem to cater to family nudity and togetherness, dedicated to just having fun in the sun. Any erotic notions one might conjure about the AANR nudist camps seem to evaporate when one doffs one's skivvies. It's generally conceded that most people look a lot better with their clothes on. In fact, when visiting a nude beach in Europe recently, Dortha and I walked along mentally dressing people.

But when it comes to sunbathing au natural, I think it should definitely be pro-choice and enjoyed by those who like to tan their fantastics in the privacy of their own camps.

In soliciting opinions from others on the subject, a quote from actress Lynn Redgrave is apropos. "We find that relaxing with clothes off at Elysium Fields (a nudist camp near Los Angeles) is a great tension reliever, for ourselves and our kids, too. We make a special point to bring our youngest with us, because we have wanted her to know from the very start that her body is good and beautiful."

Says John Money, professor emeritus at Johns Hopkins School of Medicine: "It is self-liberating to confront one's own nudity in the presence of equals at a nudist resort. Hang-ups about the body and the body image wither away. For those whose hang-ups are severe maladies, relaxation nudism is healing therapy."

And on the flip side are the immortal words from the late Erma Bombeck, who said, "If man were meant to be a nudist, they would never have invented the wicker chair."

As other nudists are quick to point out, we came into this world naked as a plucked partridge.

So, why not get the poop from the American Association for Nude Recreation, sign up, and put a little spice in your life. More than 5,000 hookup spaces abound all over the United States; chances are there's a camp near you. The next time you're moseying around in your motorcoach, drop in on the Baked Buns or the Blinking Navels.

Find out if your tastes are in line with Redgrave's or Bombeck's. For as the little nudist said when he sat on the poison ivy, "To itch his own."

Get Along Little Dogie

I had just picked up a new motorhome in Tacoma, Washington, and was heading south by myself on good old Interstate 5. More than 500 miles had clicked by since breakfast, and it was time to head for the barn.

Regrettably, I quickly discovered that I had waited too long. With absolutely no warning, a thick, gray fog suddenly enveloped my rambling ranch house. In an instant, forward visibility dropped to near zero as the damp blanket shrouded everything. I flicked off the cruise control and slowed down—not a second too soon—as I slammed on the brakes to keep from gobbling up a Datsun that had suddenly loomed ahead.

The swirling grayness was rapidly turning to deeper shades with the coming of nightfall, and I found myself hunched over the steering wheel, taut as a banjo string, as I tried to distinguish the white line on the freeway. Enough of this. When I spotted a double white line separating itself from the freeway, I nervously followed.

It led up a small rise, at the top of which a stop sign materialized out of the black void. I turned right. After several hundred yards, the pavement turned into a gravel road. The coach inched along, skittishly avoiding a fence running parallel to the road.

With the help of the spotlight, I finally found an opening in the fence. I turned in. Several squatty outbuildings dimly spotted the fog. I pulled up alongside and shut down the engine. I slumped down in my seat, completely drained. I had no idea where I was, but at least I was off that homicidal freeway.

Turning on the rig's lights, I went outside to make sure I wasn't parked on a railroad track or an airport runway. I ventured no farther than several yards, for even at this distance the well-lit rig began to dissolve in the mist. I was no stranger to thick fog, but this was ridiculous. You could not only cut it with a knife, you could make an igloo out of it. Shivering, I got back into the rig, bolted the door, and headed for the bar for a badly needed libation.

After a wee dollop or two, I still didn't know where I was, but I also didn't give a hoot. The furnace quickly dissolved the clamminess; a good stereo station dissolved the loneliness.

Completely snug in my nest, I dove into the sack of goodies my loving redhead had prepared for me and dined on cold chicken, potato salad, and gooseberry pie.

Then, smelling like a buffalo hunter as a result of the long day's activity, I decided to baptize the new bathtub. I drew a hot bath and crawled in, discovering in the process that my 6-foot 2-inch carcass folded astonishingly well into the tub. Thirty minutes later, my cares and anxieties sluiced down the drain with the spent bath water. I crawled into my pajamas, doused all but the running lights, turned down the thermostat, and zipped up my sleeping bag.

If a guy had to be stranded out in the middle of God only knows where in a dense fog, this wasn't too bad a way to do it. I wrestled with the sandman a good ten seconds before finally knuckling under to the sleep of the dead.

And then it happened. Could I be dreaming? Had the dense fog crept into my brain? I bit my lip to make sure. No, I was definitely awake. Then it happened again. The coach gave another lurch. And that sound! Of mooing—like cows. What the blazes?

I bolted out of my sleeping bag, sat up, and looked out the window. The sky was clear; a golden sun was just testing the horizon. At least the damnable fog had cleared. And then I looked down, and my heart leaped into my throat. I was surrounded by steers! I was an island in a veritable sea of wide-eyed, bawling cattle. Great balls of fire!

I raced over to the other side of the coach and pulled up the blind. I found myself staring into the stubbled face of a cowboy who was leaning over his horse to peer into the coach. I slid open the window, apparently surprising him as much as he had surprised me. "What the blazes are you doing here?" I blurted.

The cowboy stuck a Marlboro in his lips. "Came over to ask you the same question, pardner."

My gaze went beyond him to the low-lying buildings behind him.

Then it dawned. They weren't buildings at all. They were boxcars. And, at the moment, they were being stuffed with scuffling cattle being herded up their ramps by cowboys. Holy horsehockey! I had parked smack in the middle of a loading pen for cattle! In fact, had I traveled just twenty yards up the ramp in front of me, I might well have awakened in the Kansas City stockyards. My chuck wagon and I came awfully close to star billing in a Big Mac!

I slid into the driver's seat, cranked up the coach, and, without even waiting for its metabolism to rise, jammed it into gear. The rig grunted but did not move. It was moored in a sea of unground round. I put it into low gear. That didn't help. Baffled, I neutralized the gear lever to contemplate the situation.

Then, looking out over the tidal wave of T-bones, I remembered something. I reached over into the copilot's seat for my old cowboy hat. I jammed it on my head. Then I opened the window, shifted into low, and stuck my head out. "Yeeeee-ahhhhh!" I yelled. "Yaaaaa-hooooo!"

Slowly the coach started through the milling herd. I took off my hat and slapped it against the side of the coach, yelling myself hoarse. I felt like Moses at the parting of the Red Sea. A narrow chasm opened up before the on-inching rig. The Marlboro-munching cowboy came to my aid, spurring his quarter horse and helping break trail. It was slow going, the coach buffeting and groaning as it breasted the smelly leather.

Finally reaching the gate, the horseman herded the cattle away from it, opened it, and ushered me through. Safely on the other side, I thanked him. "Quite a fog last night," I said sheepishly.

"Was at that." He surveyed the rig with a critical eye. "Some dogie ya got there."

"Some dogie," I said, hooking my thumb under my cowboy hat and pushing it back on my head. I spurred the Apollo. "See ya 'round, pardner."

He gave me a three-fingered salute and closed the gate.

I drove on down the road toward the on ramp. When I was out of sight, I pulled over on a wide spot in the road. I shut down the rig, made a cup of coffee, and opened the door. Then I sat on the electric step, sipped my coffee, and gazed out at the early-morning sun climbing into the sky.

That's what we cowboys like best, I ruminated, stroking my stubble and looking out on the vista of rolling hills and mesquite. The feel of the big-country sky above us, the warm glow of coffee inside us, and—I patted the Apollo on the flanks—the feel of a good dogie beneath us. Way to go!

Introducing
Gas Guzzlers Anonymous

M ost dyed-in-the-wool RVers seem to think we aren't really motorhoming unless we put our pedal to the metal and head hellbent for Moose Mange, Alaska; Kaopectate, Mexico; Slopjar, Saskatchewan, or some other place a jillion miles from home. Not that these destinations should be missed—on the contrary. But if yo-yoing gasoline prices and the rubber-bottom recession have you hanging on the ropes, take heart. There is hope on the horizon.

For those who are hooked on long-range motorhome trips and are afraid to embark on a lengthy journey for fear the gas prices may soar to the point where you have to sell your rig to get enough money to buy gas to get home, be of good cheer. There is a solution.

I'm happy to announce the formation of a brand new organization called GGA (Gas Guzzlers Anonymous). To help frustrated long-distance RV trippers with their withdrawal symptoms, the GGA philosophy is simple: Instead of taking several gas-guzzling trips a year, it is possible to take much shorter ones and still capture the rapture of RVing.

It has to do with playing in our own backyard. Like New Yorkers who have never seen the Statue of Liberty but will fly all the way to France to see the Eiffel Tower, it is just quite possible that some very interesting things are available in our own neighborhood. Dortha and I decided to check it out. Having recently returned to our old hometown of Boise, Idaho, after being AWOL for half a century, we set out to find out if there was anything of interest in our own vicinage.

To this end we tracked down Arthur Hart. Hart is a distinguished, tall drink of sarsaparilla, sporting a thatch of white hair and an ingratiating sense of humor stolen from Will Rogers. His most redeeming qualities are the fact that he is the historian emeritus of Idaho, and he has a pretty wife named Dee.

Figuring a state historian would know as much about our state as anyone, I approached him with my questions.

As luck would have it, Hart was about to conduct a tour of Idaho in conjunction with the state's centennial. He was escorting a busload of people, and if we promised to behave ourselves, he allowed as how we could hop aboard.

We did.

After ten days of crisscrossing our panhandled state and being informed, entertained, and feted by the foremost authority on the state of Idaho, Big Red and I emerged knowing more about our old stomping ground than anyone since Lewis and Clark. Little did we realize what fascinating things went on in our own bailiwick.

It is not the purpose of this treatise to extol the virtues of Idaho. This has been done to excess of late, and as a result we are seeing the population rising much too fast. Instead, it is an endeavor to open our readers' eyes to the many fascinating spots that exist in one's own home state in which to tether an RV, whether it be in Arizona or Wisconsin.

For instance, we were amazed to find that just a few gallons away from Boise was Idaho City, a neat little ghost town that headquartered one of the largest gold sources ever discovered, with a great old cemetery that would bring drool to the lips of Alfred Hitchcock.

A ham sandwich farther on is the Sawtooth National Recreation Area, where mountain peaks touch the azure sky in splendor that is seemingly unmatched in the world. There are more great white-water rafting trips here than you can shake a wet T-shirt at. Still farther on are lakes Pend Oreille and Coeur d'Alene, so beautiful that God takes his showers there, and the latter so big that it served as a submarine navy base during World War II.

In other directions lie Hells Canyon, home of the Snake River that has carved the deepest gorge in the nation, and the mighty Salmon, nicknamed the "River of No Return." In still another direction close by is Sun Valley, a world-class resort where one may go skiing or hunting while holding hands with the ghosts of Gary Cooper and Ernest Hemingway.

Without hocking the family jewels to fill the tanks of our motorized manor, we can visit splendiferous country up to its pine cones in natural hot-water spas, rivers where you have to fight fish to keep them out of the boat, and forests that shelter all manner of feathered and furry creatures just dying to jump into your Dutch oven.

And throughout all of this pristine beauty, Idaho has liberally sprinkled campgrounds and RV parks so all of this splendor may be enjoyed by everyone—whether angler, hunter, bird-ogler, or nature lover. And now that Big Red and I have had an overview of this magnificent hunk of real estate, we can plan our RV trips to really spend some time visiting our nearby highlights of interest.

Every state has its own beauties and marvels, and there is probably no better time than now to check out one's own playground. Whether you do it with the help of your state historical office, tourist bureau, or library, you will find nearby spots of interest that you never even knew existed. And with the help of your handy dandy copy of *Trailer Life's Campground/RV Park & Services Directory*, you can find the closest campground in which to plant your sewer hose.

So if you are going through withdrawal pangs because you cannot afford to ship your rig across the Pacific Ocean for a tour of the Australian Outback this year, just start a local chapter of the GGA. You'll have no problem finding old buddies to commiserate with, right in your own purlieu.

Or, you are welcome to join our chapter. Instead of motorhoming through Siberia this year, we are going to toot down the road apiece. There's a fascinating spot named the Craters of the Moon National Monument not far from here. People from all over the world flock to see its weird lava formations, where the astronauts trained for their moon walk.

Since it's only about half-a-thermos of coffee away, maybe it's time we did.

Grass may always be greener over the septic tank, but it's not always greener on the other side of the fence. So, let's raise our coffee mugs on high for a toast to the new banner of Gas Guzzlers Anonymous—and a closer look at our own side of the fence.

Couldn't hurt.

Gallopin' Gas Gobblers

Climbing out of the Kansas flatlands into the rising range-lands of Colorado, Rocinante took the ascension in good humor. Then, on an exceptionally steep hill, I heard a honking behind us.

We were in the slow lane, so I stuck my hand out of the window and motioned for the honker to pass. As I did, a black-and-white Volkswagen sputtered past. I idly eyeballed the passing car, then suddenly felt my hackles rise. "Well, I'll be hanged!" I said to my wife. "Did you see that?"

"See what?" asked the roommate, looking up from her needlepoint.

"That VW that just passed. A woman on the passenger side gave me the finger!"

"She what?"

"The finger!" I demonstrated. "She gave me the finger!"

She slapped my hand. "I know what the finger is. Why in the world would she do that?"

"Beats me. I was hugging the right side of the road. They had plenty of room to pass."

She tried to peer through the curtain of black exhaust. "Can't make out the numbers, but it looks like a California license plate."

"Figures." I shoved back and forth in my seat, trying to coax more speed from the low-geared engine. "They would have to pass us on this steep hill. Now we'll never catch 'em."

"So, relax. They're just smart-aleck kids. Sticks and stones will break your bones, but a finger will never hurt you. Simmer down and forget it."

"It really gripes me!"

A half hour later we were peaking a long hill coming into Limon, Colorado, and I had all but dismissed the incident. Then I saw something that fanned my embers. Up ahead, pulled off at the side of the road, was the black-and-white VW, its hood lifted in the distress signal. Lounging against it was a young man wearing an army-surplus shirt and frayed Levi's; a beaded headband held shoulder-length hair out of his eyes. He held out a laconic thumb in the hitchiker's position.

"Hot damn! Do you see what I see?" I asked the wife, pulling onto the shoulder of the road.

"Looks like your friends."

"Sure does." I pulled up behind the VW.

"What are you going to do?"

"Looks like our friends are in trouble. I'm gonna lend a hand, soon as I get the tire-thumper."

"Andy Anderson! You're not going out there and start something with those kids."

Deaf to her protestations, I swung out of Rocinante with tire thumper in hand. The man started toward me. Then, as if seeing something distasteful, he turned to retrace his steps. I followed him, sizing him up as I advanced. He appeared to be college age, as did the long-haired blonde girl peering at me from the passenger side of the VW.

"Hi, there," I said.

"Hi," said the youth, leaning back against the car and casting nervous glances at the tire-thumper.

"You had your thumb out. Got a problem?"

"Well . . . uh . . . I . . . "

"Maybe I can help." I moved to the passenger side and looked in at the blonde staring up at me. "Your friend here gave me the thumb," I said, addressing her. "That I understand. But about twenty miles back, you gave me the finger, young lady. That I do not understand. Would you care to explain?"

The young man shot a threatening look at the blonde, then turned pleading eyes on me. "Look, sir, there must be some mistake. Milly doesn't go around . . . "

"Oh, Mike, shuddup!" interrupted the blonde, cutting him off with her eyes. She turned to me. "I gave you the finger."

"I know. Did you learn that in charm school?"

"I gave you the finger for good reason." She jerked her thumb toward Rocinante and said, "Because you drive that big gas-guzzling hog. Don't you know we have an energy crisis in this country? Every decent-minded citizen is trying to conserve energy, and you drive around in that big, galloping whorehouse burning up oceans of precious gasoline. You rich bastards make me wanna puke."

Taken aback, I looked at Mike. His eyes swept heavenward, beseeching assistance. I looked back into the intent brown eyes of the young woman. "Are you finished?"

"I've said all I care to say."

"Good. Now may I say a few words in my own defense before you hang and gut me?"

She answered with a silent look of disdain.

"Let's take it from the top. I'm not a rich bastard—far from it. So let's talk about energy conservation. I've done my homework, and energy studies prove that RVs save energy. The average household uses about twenty-three kilowatt hours of electricity a day. An RV on the road consumes about four kilowatt hours. RVs use no natural gas or fuel oil, and they use only a small amount of propane gas.

"Therefore, my galloping whorehouse, as you so poetically put it, uses one-fifth the energy that a house would use. In weather extremes, the savings rise dramatically because the area to be heated or air-conditioned is a tiny fraction of that in a house."

"Figures may not lie," she said smugly, "but liars can sure figure."

"Also, did you know that flushing the john at a home uses about six gallons of water? An RV uses a small fraction of that."

"I notice," she said, "you are not mentioning the gasoline that monstrosity burns."

"It's true. The rig consumes its share of gasoline while traveling. But not much more than a big car or pickup that's out of tune, which most are. Most RVs spend a lot more time sitting than traveling. And it sure as blazes doesn't use as much oil as that smog machine you're riding in. If you want to champion a cause so badly, why not tackle air pollution? You can start by cleaning up your act."

She looked at me, her eyes blazing. "I'll tackle any cause that I feel like."

"Good girl." I turned to Mike. "You're out of oil, right?"

Mike gave me a sheepish grin. "I was just going to hitchhike into town to get a couple of cans."

"Just happen to have a couple of cans in my energy-squandering whorehouse." I turned to Milly and stuck out my hand. "You've given me a finger, now how about a hand. Peace?"

She gave me a look that scorched my eyebrows, then crossed her arms and stared straight ahead.

I reclaimed my hand. "Nice talking to you, Milly." I turned to Mike. "Come with me."

He followed me over to the coach. I pulled a couple cans of oil out of the storage bin and handed them to him. He reached into his pocket. "I want to pay for these."

I stopped him. "It's on me."

He nodded, shifting uneasily "Look, sir, I want to apologize for Milly. She's a little cause-oriented. Thinks she's another Gloria Steinem."

"Hell hath no fury like a radical fem-libber."

He thanked me warmly and headed back toward his car.

I crawled back into my seat and gave the spurs to Rocinante.

"Well, dear," I said, pulling back onto the highway, "chalk one up for your lovable old husband."

"So you really got that blonde straightened out."

"That I did."

"Splendid. May I ask you one question?"

"You may."

"When you drove off, why did she give you the finger?"

Insure in Sure Insurance

Most of us approach the subject of insurance with the same lip-smacking anticipation that we contemplate a rectal root canal. The subject is confusing, expensive, frustrating, and, in general, just not a bucket of yuks. For this reason, unhappily, many of us choose to give it short shrift.

I once sold insurance when I was a lad (didn't everyone?) and got my first reactions to the ennui with which young people contemplate their future. I was not a bad insurance salesman, if I do say so myself. I managed to euchre out many innocents with such snappy phrases as, "Insure in sure insurance," "Hot cash for cold ash," "Big checks for little wrecks," and my clincher life-insurance motto: "People are dying to use our lay-away plan."

But, alas, my insurance career was short-lived. I made the mistake of insuring the new uniforms of our high-school band the year we had the worst cloudburst in history. Our company had to shell out a bundle because the uniforms shrunk, and the principal wasn't all that excited about the band showing up at the football game wearing shorts.

Then the following year, after selling every farmer in the county crop insurance, we had the worst drought in history. When my boss told me he would double my salary if I'd just go to work for the competition, it was such a blow to my pride that I retired from the insurance business forever. As far as selling insurance, with my luck I'd invest in a pumpkin farm and they would do away with Halloween.

However, this experience, although frustrating, did provide an unforgettable lesson in the importance of proper insurance planning, which I have never forgotten. A couple of recent incidents have underscored the wisdom of reviewing one's insurance policies from time to time.

The first incident was a terrible tragedy suffered by one of *MotorHome*'s favorite columnists, Gaylord Maxwell, when his new motorhome caught fire. Says Gaylord, "Near midnight on a cold, lonely stretch of Interstate 65 south of Nashville, Tennessee, we stood helplessly and watched our new rig and its contents burn to the ground. We were left with only our towed car and the clothes on our backs."

So that other people may profit from his misfortune, Gaylord goes on to state that all RVers—especially full-time motorhomers—should carry large fire extinguishers, provide fireproof boxes for their vital papers, subscribe to the Good Sam Emergency Road Service, pre-plan fire emergency procedures, and carry replacement-value insurance.

Expounding on the latter, Gaylord states, "After a disaster is not the time to plan insurance. Fortunately, in our case, we had excellent coverage, so our financial loss was minimal. Excellent coverage means replacement of the rig or compensation for its real value at today's prices for everything lost. The term 'replacement' is crucial. Without it, compensation may be at very reduced, prorated figures."

Being a learned man of the letters and a seasoned RVer, Gaylord was well-prepared for his emergency— insurance-wise— when his rig caught fire that harrowing night.

The other recent incident that underlines the importance of proper insurance planning happened to two old friends,

LaVerne and Joannie Huff. LaVerne was an optometrist practicing in Santa Clara, California. Approaching his golden years, and suddenly realizing there was more to life than peering into strange eyeballs, LaVerne decided to take down his shingle and take up the life of a full-time RVer. So he and Joannie sold their house, bought a brand-new Fleetwood Bounder, and moved in bag and baggage.

Joy reigned supreme until it was time to leave the new motorhome at the repair shop for some warranty work. Joannie picked up the narrative when the repair shop called to say, "Dr. Huff, your motorhome is gone!"

"Well," said Joannie, "I can't imagine any more chilling words than to hear that your motorhome has been stolen. We couldn't believe our ears."

With the shock slowly being replaced by anger, the Huffs filled out the police reports. Then, said Joannie, "Since we were standing in everything we owned, we had to buy toothbrushes, underwear, clothes, etc., to carry on. I didn't fall apart or get hysterical. I was too mad. How dare they!"

About a week later, the savaged motorhome was found by the police on top of Pacheco Pass, about fifty miles away. Adds Joannie, "The inside was a mess. There had been wine spilled on the rug . . . broken cabinets where the television and microwave used to be . . . nothing left in the compartments, drawers, nothing!

"There was a big bucket in the front part of the coach with gasoline in it. The consensus was they were going to torch it but decided not to. I almost wish they had, because it will never be my sweet little house again. How awful to think someone had slept on my bed and touched my refrigerator and used my potty. Ugh! I want it fumigated!"

Even sadder was the fact that the coach was insured, but there was some question as to the coverage of its contents. As virtually everything they owned had been stowed in the coach for full-time living, this would amount to a terrible loss if their insurance proved inadequate.

When you consider you're having that romantic candlelight dinner in a small confinement that also houses very large tanks containing many gallons of gasoline and propane, it's wise to carefully plan insurance coverage. And when you consider that your home and all its contents can be spirited away by a hot-wire expert, it's not exactly stupid to carry theft insurance.

Happily, the chances of being a victim of fire or theft is about the same as your chances of winning the Bangladesh lottery. But the fact remains, it does happen.

So sit down right now, and dig out your insurance policies. Make sure that you're not only fully covered on your rig, but on all of its contents as well—and covered by replacement-value insurance. Then make a list of all the contents of your motorhome, right down to the can opener, and put the list in a safe place other than in your rig.

There are some other things you can do. I always have a propane sniffer and a smoke alarm in my rig, even though the latter does alert everyone in camp when I'm making toast. And some RVers paint a number in huge letters on top of their rig, so it could be identified by a sheriff's chopper from the air in case it is stolen.

But the thrust of this chapter is insurance. When you're sifting through ashes is no time to wonder about your coverage. So check it out right now, hear? Or I'll sic my wife on you. And there's no insurance against redheads.

"Attend a Samboree? You Crazy?"

It is no secret that this scribe is generally regarded as having a dipstick that shows he's about a quart low. This is true. I readily admit to being a devout, card-carrying paranoid. It's not that I don't love people. I do. But I love them in very small groups. Like one on one.

I have been known to pass up an elevator with more than two people on board, and I'm like the gent who quit going to football games because he knew the guys out there in the huddle were saying nasty things about him.

So what was a lug who doesn't even like two-handed solitaire doing at a Samboree? And not only a Samboree, but an *international* Samboree? With almost 2,000 RVs in attendance? Good question. Let's take it from the top.

After the memsahib and I elected to return to our old hometown of Boise, Idaho, we sold our home, cranked up Rocinante, galloped north, and lived in our ubiquitous wheel estate while building our home in Boise.

Since the whole state of Idaho contains fewer people than the Sacramento metropolitan area, there's lots of elbow room here. To an Idahoan, the great outdoors is not just a phrase, it's a way of life. There are probably more RVs of every description, per capita, in Idaho than anyplace else in the United

States—and more beautiful places to plug one into. Ranking right up there with Alaska, there's no place with more beautiful, remote, uncrowded scenery than can be enjoyed from the front stoop of one's motorhome, parked in the Gem State.

You can imagine, therefore, the culture shock that reverberated throughout the Anderson household when we learned that our idyllic existence was about to be shattered by the arrival of some 4,000 RVers, celebrating their annual foofaraw. The Good Sam River Run International Samboree was a five-day dry camp to be held at the Western Idaho Fairgrounds. Not only was this invasion of gallivanting gypsies coming to our hometown, the fairgrounds were practically in our backyard!

For a family who had taken to RVing for the last three decades mainly because it offered a chance to get out and away from the madding crowd, we were about to become involved with a great gaggle of axle geese who actually enjoyed the company of huge flapping flights of other RVers.

Considering this a good time to take that long-awaited trip to Zimbabwe, Dortha was negotiating with our travel agent when we got a strange request. Would I consider holding an autograph party to sign copies of our latest travel book about RVing in Alaska? Since a lot of RVers would be in attendance who had expressed interest in an Alaskan adventure, it would be a thoughty thing to do.

If there's anything I hate worse than congregations, it's autograph parties. Ever since holding a book-signing session with Erma Bombeck in Phoenix one time at which she sold three freight cars full of her books and I sold six copies of mine (to relatives), this did not have a salubrious effect on my paranoia. My proposed negative answer, however, was debated by my better half. She insisted that it might be of interest to attend a Samboree, just so we would know what all the fuss was about.

Besides, it would certainly make good grist for the column. Knowing where my "bed was bruttered," I put Zimbabwe on hold and reluctantly acquiesced. I mentally geared myself for the worst, which I was sure would be indescribable. Then, as the covered wagons started to arrive from all corners of the earth and gather in a circle, I received a calendar of events. My jaw dropped. Less planning had gone into the Normandy Beach invasion. The schedule offered seminars, lectures, tours, clinics, games, teas, entertainment, square dancing, and even a grandma's brag session.

You could learn the latest on making the most of your microwave oven, how to run your RV on solar energy, flycasting for the wily trout, fulltiming in your RV, or the proper care and feeding of your copilot.

You could take tours ranging from white-water rafting to scouting Hell's Canyon to studying wild birds in their native habitat.

The piddling registration fee entitled Good Samers to free kaffeeklatsches, lunches, pancake breakfasts, and ice-cream socials. It even offered a health fair in conjunction with a local hospital that provided screening for blood pressure, glaucoma, diabetes, vision, hearing, and cholesterol, not to mention a foot-care clinic for those who tried to take in everything.

But most impressive was the entertainment. There was square dancing, the Serendipity Singers, a top-notch "King of Swing" band, the Showtimers, Oinkari Basque Dancers, the famous Ruwe Family Band, the Golden Knights Army Parachute Team, and my old secret passion: Kay Starr. Truly, a lineup that would make Vegas look to its laurels.

So, my curiosity temporarily subjugating my paranoia, I attended the opening ceremonies. Instead of surging crowds, I was surprised to see groups of attendees in clusters, the clusters being distinguished by bright tartan colors of their Good Sam vests designating their chapters. With representatives from all the states, this colorful mosaic made the grandstand a fascinating giant patchwork quilt.

And from the impressive opening ceremonies to the final door-prize drawing day, I found myself feeling more and more comfortable with this laid-back, mostly retired, easygoing class of Homo sapiens. The Good Samers, even in bunches, were good-natured, friendly, nicely tanned from being outdoors and genuinely concerned about their fellow man. They seemed to take their Good Samaritan logo to heart.

I even attended their flea market, a lively bazaar at which everyone sells useless things to each other, and found that even this babble did not bring out uncontrollable claustrophobia.

In sum, we had a ball. This is not to say the frau and I have eschewed the untrammeled solitude of a beautiful mountain park. There's a lot to be said for brook babbling and silence echoing. But it did open our eyes to the attraction of a Samboree for the first time. I guess we all are basically a people who just naturally enjoy the company of other people. And when you can get a group of people who are enjoying the same pursuits, lifestyles, and entertainment together, why shouldn't they have a blast?

Needless to say, I have renewed my Good Sam membership. In fact I'll probably go to the next international Samboree.

Oh yes, I did autograph some books. My relatives from California showed up.

Billy Joe Bob Slept Here

It was on one of my rare motorhome trips traveling alone, and I had swung into the rest area just north of Eugene, Oregon. I was returning from a trip to the restroom when the sound of amplified guitar music assailed my eardrums.

Searching for its source, I spotted a brand new luxury motorhome that had pulled up alongside Rocinante. A large FOR SALE sign had been scrawled on butcher's paper and taped to the outside of the coach. I stood for a moment, my eyes forming question marks, when a young, attractive brunette popped out of the door and bounced toward me. "Interested in buying a gallivantin' wigwam?"

I watched the young lady, whose long, ribboned braids on both sides of her head jiggled with her tank top in tune to a pair of jeans so tight they twanged. I cleared my throat. "Afraid not, miss." I pointed to the Dolphin. "One of these things is about all I can handle. Don't know what I'd do with two."

"Know whatcha mean." She took another bite of the carrot she was munching and squinted up at me. "Well, have a good day."

I stopped her as she started to turn back. "May I ask why you're selling that beautiful new Cambria?"

"Sure thing. Billy Joe Bob decided he doesn't want anything to do with a pad on wheels, ya know?"

"Who is Billy Joe Bob? A trio?"

I received a pained look. "You mean you never heard of Billy Joe Bob?" She nodded toward the coach. "That's him playin' now. In person." I listened for a moment to the amplified guitar that was surely being scored on the Mount Palomar seismograph. "Don't say you never heard of Billy Joe Bob?"

"I'll never say it again. Believe me."

"He's got a bullet on the charts."

"A bullet on the charts. That's good?"

I received another look of disdain. "Next you'll say you never heard Billy Joe Bob's big single, 'I Want You So Bad I Can Taste It, Which Is Why I Gave Up Chewing Tobacco.'"

"Oh, *that* Billy Joe Bob."

She somehow managed to grin and jiggle at the same time. "Costs twenty bucks to hear him in concert, ya know. You're hearing him for nothin'. How does that grab ya ?"

"Makes me feel good all over," I said, sincerely hoping the bullet didn't shatter Rocinante's windshield, "but you haven't answered my question. Why're you selling your RV?"

She took another bite of her carrot. "Well, buyin' it was Billy Joe Bob's idea, ya know? He wanted to live in it while on tour. He's got this awful hangup about Holiday Inns, ya know? But it didn't work out."

"Why not? Lots of entertainers are using RVs to get around to their concert gigs."

"Billy Joe Bob's kinda different, ya know? He's gonna be the world's hottest country-western star. But handy around the house he ain't. Would ya like a ferinstance?"

"Please."

"Well, we just bought this rig last month, ya know? First night we parked near Big Sur, right on the ocean. Sure did have a jim-dandy time. That is, 'til the tide came in. We woke up with two feet of water coverin' the floor. Had to have a tractor come yank us out. I told Billy Joe Bob we didn't have to park that close to the ocean, ya know? But he wouldn't listen." She giggled. "That Billy Joe Bob's more dang fun."

"So that's why you're selling the Cambria?"

"Oh, no. That was just the first night. The second night we parked up in the mountains near Carmel. Billy Joe Bob gave up tryin' to get the rig level, so he decided it would be more romantic to sleep on an angle anyway. Which was all right, but while fixin' dinner, I opened the oven door and watched an apple pie and a ten-pound turkey skate right out of the oven, across the floor, and down a twenty-two-foot cliff." She sighed at the memory. "Sure did taste awful when we finally found it."

"I see. No wonder you're selling the motorhome."

"Oh, no. That's not why. The third night Billy Joe Bob thought he might have better luck tryin' an RV park. So he pulled into one near Monterey. It was real crowded, and we were right proud of the way he squeezed that big rig right through all that traffic." She nibbled her carrot. "Then it happened."

"What happened?"

"Billy Joe Bob didn't know he'd left the TV antenna cranked up. That is, 'til he hit the power line. Sure did liven things up for a while. Especially when all the lights in the park blew out. Not to mention what it did to his geetar amplifier."

"My God! I don't blame you for wanting to sell your rig."

"Oh, that's not why we're selling it."

I looked at her aghast. "You mean there's more?"

She nodded. "The next morning, Billy Joe Bob pulled out and forgot to do one little thing."

"One little thing?"

"Yep. He forgot to unhook the water hose. Would you believe we heard that awful ruckus and looked back to see we were draggin' a hundred feet of plumbing, a pop-up Volkswagen, and a wash basin from the women's john?"

"Now wait a minute. I find this just a bit hard to swallow."

"So that's why we're sellin' the rig. As I said, Billy Joe Bob ain't all that handy around the house."

"You mean to tell me . . ."

"But you gotta admit, Billy Joe Bob's more gol-danged fun!" She cupped her ear. "Listen to that! Didja ever hear anybody make a geetar talk like that?"

I listened, hoping my eardrums would hang in tough. "He's not bad at making it shout, either," I managed over the din. "Well, it's certainly been nice talking to you."

"Nice talkin' to you, too, ya know?"

"Hope you sell your coach."

"We'll sell it. Lotsa people want the house Billy Joe Bob slept in." She waved her carrot top at me. "Bye." Then she twanged her jeans back into the coach and shut the door behind her.

I hurried into the quieter confines of Rocinante and gratefully closed the door. As I waited for my ears to quit ringing, I thought of what the pretty brunette had said. Obviously, living in an RV isn't for everyone; it is not a universal emollient for rat-race-itis.

Especially if your name is Billy Joe Bob, you play the guitar, and you ain't too handy around the house.

The Cemetery

It's not too often that one encounters a woman who waxes her mustache. Even in the state of Wyoming.

We were gassing up at a Rock Springs service station when I happened to notice the old dusty camper parked next to Rocinante. "Howdy," said a husky voice emanating from the pickup.

I looked into the craggy face of the elderly woman peering out at me from under a fly-bedecked fishing hat. "Evening, ma'am," I replied.

"Overheard you askin' the gas attendant for a place to park for the night."

"Right. It's been a long day. We're ready to put the nose bag on our beast."

"Then jest follow me. I'll show you the best spot in these parts."

I finished gassing up, paid the attendant, and buckled into the cockpit. Scratching gravel, the camper started up and shot out of the station, the woman waving out of the window for us to follow. As she drove off, we noticed the sticker on her rear bumper reading PRESERVE WYOMING WILDLIFE—SHOOT AN OUT-OF-STATE HUNTER. I looked at my wife. "Think we should follow her?"

She shrugged. "What have we got to lose? I'm tired."

It took some doing to keep up with the camper as we drove through Rock Springs, then turned up a country road for a few miles. The camper finally blinked its left-turn signal, and we followed as it turned off the road and rattled through an open gate. We were almost through the entrance before we saw the sign.

"Good Lord!" exclaimed Dortha. "This is a cemetery! Where in the world is she taking us?"

"Or out of this world?"

The old camper pulled over to the side of the road and parked in a tree-shaded lane. I pulled up behind and stopped. The woman bounded out of the cab and ran over to our rig.

"Slicker'n moose dung, ain't it?" she said, beaming expansively.

"Nice," I said. "But I do have one question. What the blazes are we doing here?"

"Pitchin' camp, pardner. What else?"

"You mean right here? In this marble orchard?"

"You betcha. Don't sit there flappin' yer gums. Time to put on the feedbag." She addressed the redhead. "Got a venison roast cooking. You set the table, dearie, while I whip up some biscuits."

"You have a roast cooking?" asked Dortha.

"Yep. Should be about done. Come on. We'll take a gander at it." Before the wife could protest, she found herself being propelled toward the camper. Amused, I followed, as the woman went to the front of her rig and unlatched the engine hood. She took an old pair of mittens out of her mackinaw, put them on, and reached inside the engine well to come out with a large object wrapped in aluminum foil. "Aha!" she said, sniffing it. "Smells larrupin' good."

Dortha blinked for a moment, then finally mustered the courage to ask, "What smells larrupin' good?"

"Supper," said the woman. "Don't tell me you ain't never done any motorblock cooking?"

"I'm afraid I haven't," said Dortha, peeling back the foil and sniffing. "But it smells heavenly."

"Only way inna world to cook venison. This was kind of an old buck, so I seasoned the roast up good, sealed it in this here foil, and put it on the motorblock. No use lettin' all that engine heat go to waste. Best oven inna world." She sniffed again. "Not bad for road kill."

"I've never heard of such a thing," said Dortha, entranced. "How long do you cook it?"

"Old duffer like this, ya cook it about a hundred and twenty miles." She headed for the door of the camper throwing back, "Come on, mule skinners. Wash up for supper. Let's look alive."

I looked over at my bride. She watched the retreating woman, then swept the marbled plots with puzzled eyes, finally planting them on me. "Let's look alive?"

It isn't every night one has a banquet in a graveyard, and it turned out to be a very interesting evening. Over venison so tender you could cut it with a fork, we fell in love with Babe Singer, even though she chewed snuff and wore a T-shirt that said I'M A VIRGIN on the front and THIS IS AN OLD T-SHIRT on the back. She was a product of Saddlestring, Wyoming, where she and her husband had run a hunting lodge for many years, until Cecil died following a misunderstanding with a grizzly bear. After Cecil's demise, Babe couldn't stand being around the lodge "without the old coot," so she sold out, bought the camper, and has been cemetery-hopping ever since.

"They don't come any weirder'n me, honey," said Babe, tucking a pinch of Copenhagen under her upper lip. She jerked her head toward a double-barreled 12-gauge racked on the wall over her bed. "Somebody take a mind to bust in here uninvited, 'twould be the worst mistake he ever made."

Dortha mulled this, then asked, "Do you make a habit of staying in cemeteries?"

"Hell, yes, I guess. Can you think of a better place? They generally got lotsa shade, are nice and green."

After dinner we toasted the last frontier with a cup of coffee so strong it made holes in my Styrofoam cup, and Babe insisted on opening not only her heart to us but her giant larder as well. We went home laden with several brook trout, a venison roast, and a quart of wild huckleberries.

"What a fascinating woman," said Dortha, crawling into the goosedown.

"I'm glad you gave her our permanent address. That's one gal I'd like to meet up with again."

And then we joined our neighbors in repose, sleeping the sleep of the dead. When we awoke the next morning, the old camper was gone; very possibly Babe was stalking a grizzly bear through the Wyoming high country.

I felt a small twinge of sympathy. If this were true, that poor grizzly would never have a chance.

Shelter at the Summit

I happened to be alone in the rig, Rocinante and I returning from a short trip to Medford, Oregon. The blizzard had hit just as we were starting the slow climb over the Siskiyou Summit. At Ashland, patches of snow began to replace the drizzle; rain puddles gave way to sheets of ice. Gusts of howling wind blasted through the mountains, catching Rocinante in an icy grip that threatened to send her spinning.

As we approached the summit, the snow was getting deeper, and cars were beginning to dot the sides of the road. The Dolphin plowed on, its big duals gripping the icy road with authority, its huge windshield wipers combating the slush with defiance, the defrosters dispelling the steam that oozed from nervous pores.

It was with relief that I finally saw the headlights pick up the white-mantled sign along the freeway announcing Siskiyou Summit. Now, if the downhill side wasn't snow clogged, Rocinante and I might successfully negotiate the last hurdle between us and home. I pulled over behind several parked trucks to celebrate with a cup of coffee.

I was just lighting the stove burner when I heard tapping at the door. With some effort, I pushed the door open against the icy blast. There, looking more like an apparition than a human being, was a slight figure holding onto a cowboy hat and a serape that was flapping wildly in the wind.

"*S-s-señor*," the words were barely audible above the thunder of the storm, "I need help."

"Come in, *amigo*."

"*M-m-muchas gracias*," stammered the little Mexican, stomping the snow off his feet as he entered. He took off his hat and twisted it in his hands, anguish showing in his eyes. "I have beeg problem, *señor*." He pointed at the road up ahead. "My peekup ees *muerto*."

"*Muerto*?" I slid my finger across my throat. "You mean dead?"

His head nodded vigorously. "*Sí, sí*. And my *familia ees muy frio*. I got beeg worry, *señor*."

"Go get 'em," I said, "before they freeze to death."

"Ah, *Dios mio, señor. Muchas gracias!*" He started crossing himself.

"Don't stand there. Git!" I all but threw him out the door.

With the engine's heater shut down, it was getting chilly in the coach. I turned on the furnace, and by the time I got a pan of water on the stove and the burner lit, hot air was coming out of the furnace ducts.

Answering the knock at the door, I admitted the Mexican family. The man came in first, followed by his shivering wife, and then my astonished eyes saw five stair-step kids bringing up the rear. None of them had any warm clothing, and the smallest—a snippet of a girl with big brown eyes and trembling blue lips—could barely climb the steps. I picked her up and sat her down in front of the furnace register, where she sat, surveying me as if I were Santa Claus.

"Get comfortable," I said to the group. "I'm sorry the galley isn't stocked, but I do have some hot chocolate and some breakfast rolls. We'll heat them up and see if we can thaw you all out."

"*Gracias, señor,*" said the diminutive mother. "*Muchas gracias.*"

"*Por nada,*" I said, exhausting my Spanish vocabulary. "My pleasure." Unnesting a stack of Styrofoam cups, I poured the hot chocolate and passed it around. Each of the children took a cup as if it were the Holy Grail and sat holding it, reveling in its warmth, sniffing its aroma. As I handed out the breakfast rolls, I couldn't help but notice the expression on the mother's face. I fought a tinge of guilt as her wide eyes embraced the sumptuousness of the warm coach, which had provided sudden and unexpected succor to her family—an oasis of food and warmth in the teeth of an angry blizzard that moments before had seriously threatened their very lives.

I sat down by the father and stuck out my hand. "Name's Anderson."

The little man rose and bowed, removing his cowboy hat. "I am Manuel Garcia, *señor.*" He clasped my hand in both of his. "You are a saint, *Señor* Anderson. You are answer to my prayers."

I chuckled. "A saint? That'll be the day. I just happened to be passing by. You'd have done the same for me. Now I think we'd better get moving. The snow is getting deeper, and the longer we wait the tougher it's going to be. I'll take your family to Yreka. You can stay there until the storm blows over, then you can come back and get your pickup."

He nodded his head. "*Si, señor. Bueno. Bueno.*" I crawled into the cockpit, motioning for Garcia to climb into the copilot seat. He virtually leaped into it, his eyes the size of tortillas. I cranked the engine and moved out into the deepening snow.

I was not a very good host for the next hour, being completely preoccupied with getting Rocinante down below the snow level. The snow presented few problems, but the long stretches of ice always appeared hand in glove with the blasts of crosswinds that propelled the huge machine as if it were a spinnaker sail, making for some lively moments in the cockpit. Approaching Yreka, however, things calmed down as the cold front passed, the wind abated, and the snow turned back into drizzle. Relaxing a bit, I turned to Mañuel Garcia and engaged him in conversation.

It turned out that he was a "peeker of the fruit" and was belatedly heading south for the winter because of an illness in the family. He was on his way to the San Joaquin Valley in Central California and was rejoicing in the fact that his three oldest kids were now big enough to help in the fields.

"Someday" he said, running his palms over the upholstered captain's chair, "the family of Manuel Garcia weel have a rolling *casa* like thees."

"I hope so," I said, smiling at him. "I sincerely hope so."

Taking the Yreka off ramp, I followed the signs to the California Highway Patrol station. I talked to the patrolman at the desk, explaining the situation. He was most sympathetic, saying he would be happy to see that the Garcias were taken care of and, when the storm lifted, a trooper would return them to their pickup.

Back at the motorhome, I relayed the information to the Garcia family, and they filed out, each of the brood shaking my hand and giving me a well-rehearsed speech of thanks in Spanish. When the little tyke came out, she reached up her arms and I picked her up to receive a tight hug and a wet kiss on the cheek. Her mother, eyes damp, took my hand in hers.

"*Vaya con Dios*," she said.

"*Y tú*," I said. "And good luck, Mrs. Garcia."

Her husband brought up the rear. "*Muchas gracias, Señor* Anderson. I hope again we will meet."

"I would like that, Mr. Garcia." I offered him my hand, with a greenback folded in the palm. He shook it, then looked questioningly at the bill.

"What is this, *señor?*"

"Very little. I thought it might buy a hamburger for your family."

He shoved it back into my hand, a pained expression on his face. "*No, gracias, Señor. Tengo mucho dinero.*"

He patted his wallet pocket. "*Mucho dinero.*"

I knew he lied. I also knew his pride would not be bought for a lousy twenty bucks. I put the bill back in my pocket. "*Adios, amigo.*"

He herded his brood into the station, then turned before following them inside. He waved. "*Adios, señor.*"

The Schoolteachers

Our leisurely sojourn across the great Northwest had been rudely interrupted by a movie producer, who allowed as how my presence was sorely needed in Hollywood to revise a screenplay I had written on the legendary hero of the Flying Tigers, General Claire Chennault.

Miffed at having our motorhome trip aborted, the thought of stabling Rocinante on the floor of the San Fernando Valley in the middle of a Southern California summer did little to boost our morale. My protestations were finally stifled, however, by the promise of a very large check.

Accordingly, we soon found ourselves plugged into a nice RV park just outside the city limits of Los Angeles, using Rocinante as a home base while I set up my word cruncher and started to work. We were quick to discover that traveling in a motorhome is one thing; living in it is something else again, especially when my computer gear shared the front room with a nervous movie producer and a director who kept pulling pages out of the word processor. And in no time at all, we were to learn that the most efficient air-conditioner is no match for the temperatures of the San Fernando Valley, which can send the mercury squirting right out the top of its tube.

Not that it was much solace, but Big Red and I were not suffering in solitude. We had pulled in next door to the smallest travel trailer on two wheels. So small, in fact, its method of locomotion was a 1956 Volkswagen. When we first observed the diminutive rig, we figured it could only be inhabited by a covey of elves or, at best, a set of newlywed dwarfs.

To my amazement, when the owners showed up after work our first night in camp, I found myself looking up into the face of a friendly fellow who extended at least six feet, six inches into the smog. His wife, a very pretty young lady, also sniffed the rarer climes from a six-foot advantage. Together they made a striking, if very large-framed, picture.

I hoisted the martini flag at the proper time, and the couple joined us for a happy-hour libation. It developed they were both schoolteachers at California State University at Northridge and were living as cheaply as possible while building their house.

"How on earth do you two get into that tiny trailer?" asked the redhead, completely awed by anything one-third the size of her rambling residence, which was giving her increasingly frequent fits of claustrophobia.

"We don't get into it," said the attractive young wife. "We just sort of put it on."

"Right," agreed her husband. "And right about now it's beginning to get a little tight in the crotch."

"Charley!" admonished his wife. "We'll be out of it one of these days," she said, planting a large palm over her mate's mouth. "We've just about finished our little dream cottage in Sherman Oaks."

"Marvelous," said the missus.

"Tell the Andersons what happened the other day," said the bride, smiling at her husband. "I think they might enjoy a funny story."

"By all means," I said.

"You mean last weekend?" he asked, removing his wife's palm.

"Yes."

A broad grin split Charley's features. "All right." He primed himself with a large gulp from his martini. "You see, folks, we spend every weekend working on our new house. We're doing the painting ourselves. We just hitch up the trailer, drive over, and park it in our driveway. Last weekend we took off as usual, with Fran driving. I decided to ride in the trailer and clean some paintbrushes on the way.

"We were cruising along at a nice clip when suddenly we stopped. Just like that. When we didn't start right up again, I decided to get out and see what the wife had run into—or over. I no sooner got out of the trailer and started for the Volks when a long signal light changed, and Fran started up. I was left standing in the road, high and dry."

"This was an especially acute problem," said Fran, laughing, "because it was so hot in the trailer, Charley was wearing only his jockey shorts."

"This might have been a problem anywhere but in L.A.," said Charley. "But here, of course, no one even noticed me."

"What on earth did you do?" asked my missus.

"Hailed a cab. And here's the clincher: I got home before Fran, and she turned into the driveway, naturally thinking I was in the trailer. When she saw me lying on the chaise lounge in front of the house, drinking a bottle of beer, it so surprised her that she drove right through the garage door." He pointed at the Volkswagen. "Would you like to have a good buy on a Volks with a snub nose?"

Needless to say, we became quite attached to the young couple, and they did much to relieve our knotty situation in the hot months ahead. Their new house was finally finished, and Charley no longer had to live in a travel trailer that was a little tight in the crotch.

As for the Andersons, Big Red's eyeballs ignited one hot day, and the producer, director, writer, and computer gear were ordered out of her motorhome and told to find an office in Hollywood. This was done, and it was amazing how this simple act expanded the space in our motorhome just in time to halt divorce proceedings.

The screenplay has now gone through a dozen revisions, and the movie has yet to materialize. The same may be said for the promised very large check.

So much for amorous, glamorous Hollywood. We'd prefer to be in the company of bright young schoolteachers anytime.

The Collision

It all started when we were driving along the famous Las Vegas Strip, gazing goggle-eyed at the lush hotels that had sprung up like toadstools in a cow pasture since our last visit to Sin City.

Coming to Caesar's Palace, I decided to make a lap through the driveway just to see how this old testimony to man's debauchery was holding up. I reined Rocinante off the street and turned into the fountain-splashed driveway that leads to the hotel. While the distaff ogled the fountain statuary that guards the lush grounds in various states of undress, we cruised by the front portals. I was just turning back on the curving exit road when the crash came. It was a jolting, neck-snapping impact that seemed to have its origin somewhere in Rocinante's posterior section.

I slammed on the brakes, stopped, and quickly checked my copilot for injuries. Finding none, I told Dortha to stay in the rig, then dismounted with blood in my eye.

I found myself face to vest pocket with a massive, rough-hewn gentleman, who had also dismounted from his steed—a very large Cadillac. The Caddy, unhappily, had just completed a merger with the rear end of Rocinante. I suddenly found my right hand in an embrace with a warm, moist vice. I looked up, past an expensive Cuban cigar, into a pair of brown, bloodshot eyes that seemed to be afflicted with a slight focusing problem.

"Name's Flannigan," said deep-voiced words that had obviously been well marinated in Scotch. "Ah'm in oil."

"Correction, my friend," I said, figuring under the circumstances the best defense was a good offense, "you're in hot water."

I received a stunning slap on the back. "That's what ah like. A sense of humor. Always like to run into a man with a sense of humor."

"I'm very sorry," I said humorously, "that you had to run into this one." I went back to survey the damage. Rocinante's right rear had been violated by the rear bumper of the Cadillac, resulting in a large, gaping hole. A puddle was forming under the rear wheel, signifying our rig had suffered a compound fracture of the water tank, accompanied by severe lacerations. I resisted the urge to bend down and apply a tourniquet to the afflicted artery. "Look what you've done to our home," I said. "It's leaking."

"Sho 'nuff," said the man, laboriously getting down on all fours to survey the damage. "Ah trust that's water."

"Fortunately it is. The sewer tank's on the other side."

"Glory be!" he said, standing up. "We've always got something to be thankful fo'." I found a beefy arm had encircled my shoulders. "Mah good man, ah'm sure this whole affair can be handled to your satisfaction. It is obvious that ah was backin' out of mah parkin' place in too much of a hurry. Ah accept the blame fo' the whole incident."

"I scarcely call it an incident," I said, choking on the Cuban incinerator that was burning near my nose. "I have just traveled 8,000 miles, over the Canadian Rockies, only to get done in by a drunk in front of a 'Lost Wages' gambling den."

"Now, mah good man." The hand belonging to the beefy arm around my shoulder started patting. "Ah know exactly how you feel. But ah want to show you something." He removed his stogie and used it to point in the direction of his car. "See that?" I sighted along his cigar in the direction indicated. I noticed the blonde coiffured head in the front seat of his Cadillac. It was trying to burrow down inconspicuously into the collar of an elegant mink coat. "That," said the man in a confidential tone, "is not my wife."

"That's too bad," I said.

"Ain't it, though," he said sadly. He gave me a kittenish gouge in the kidneys with his elbow. "And ah'm not too sure mah wife would understand what she's doin' in that mink coat I just bought her."

"Some wives," I said, massaging the hole in my kidneys, "are not very understanding."

"Mine shore as heck ain't. She's lak a Texas longhorn."

My eyes watering from the noxious blend of Scotch vapors and cigar smoke, I engineered a separation from the large arm. "How would you like to handle this?"

"Ah want to handle this the Texas way, friend. But ah also would lak to do it on the q.t." A large bloodshot eye winked at me. "Fo' obvious reasons." He maneuvered his weaving bulk over to Dortha's rolled-down window. He introduced himself and apologized in grand fashion for the unfortunate mishap. "So if you-all will accept mah apologies, ah wish you would move into mah suite here in the hotel. Ah have one on a permanent basis, and we just checked out. Jest move in as mah guests while we have your li'l old chuck wagon fixed up, good as new. Would you-all do that?"

"We would," I said, giving visual signals to several bellhops who had gathered around the accident. "Our clothes are in the closet there, boys."

"We would not!" said the missus. The bellhops stopped in their tracks.

I looked at Dortha in amazement. "Honey, you obviously didn't hear. This gentleman wants us to move into his suite—in this hotel—all expenses paid!"

"I wouldn't think of it," she said. She turned to the bellhops. "Don't you touch a thing."

I looked, unbelieving, at the redhead. "Dortha, are you loco? Here's our chance for a little vacation in one of the country's swankest sin dens. Bars, floor shows, eighty-five swimming pools, bars, prize fights—"

"Andy Anderson! Shame on you. Rocinante has been wounded. She's back there now, bleeding. You would abandon her in her hour of need?"

"What?"

"This is our home. It has our personal belongings in it. And I'm not letting it out of my sight. Besides," she folded her arms, "I just bought food for a week. Now, you just thank this nice gentleman and tell him he can oblige us by making arrangements to have Rocinante fixed up at the best RV repair shop in Las Vegas."

I stared slack-jawed at my wife, then turned to the Texan. "Well, you heard the boss."

"And a pretty little filly she is," said the Texan, reaching for his wallet. "Here's mah card. You-all jest have yer rollin' bunkhouse fixed up good as new, and send me the bill."

I took the card as he turned on his heel and headed for his car, saying, "Sho' was nice runnin' into you folks."

"A real blast," I said.

And so it came to pass that instead of lolling in the lap of luxury in a fantastic hotel, we spent the next three nights parked in the lot of an RV service shop that was guarded by a night watchman who carried around a ghetto-blaster that could be heard on three continents.

I dearly love my redheaded roommate. She's the pepperoni on my pizza. But there are times when, like all women, she can be a clump of crabgrass in the lawn of life.

Salubrious Side Effects

A side from that cool, clear look of a seeker of wisdom and truth, there is another characteristic of the RV lifestyle aficionado that is very evident.

I refer, of course, to the fantastic reflex action of our typical RVer. And I don't mean just the normal knee-jerk reaction of the average person; we're talking about industrial-strength reflexes of the type that would have been the envy of Mohammed Ali, Leon Spinks, or Chuck Yeager. We're talking heavy-duty lightning-fast responses here.

Now what is there about the RV lifestyle that hones our reflexes to such a hair-trigger response—especially members of our RV fraternity who spend a lot of time in Canada? There are many reasons, but for the purpose of this précis we shall examine just a few.

As we all know, there are many attractions that draw us to the land of our friendly neighbors up north. The beauty is unsurpassed, the currency exchange is favorable, and our RVs are more than welcome in the magnificent Canadian campgrounds. About the only pimple on the face of this camping paradise is the presence of the indigenous insects.

The Canadian mosquito, as all naturalists know, is not really an insect. It is a mutation dammed by a Canadian honker and sired by the Stealth bomber. These airborne vampires have been known to carry away small children and could easily suck a person bone-white in a matter of minutes.

When our rug rats were small, we used to do a lot of camping in Canadian parks. As a result, not only did we parents refine our reflex reaction speed, but our children were indoctrinated at a very early age as well. From the first day we saw the Canadian mosquitoes wheeling down out of the sun in attack formation, we knew this was an adversary to be reckoned with.

In all fairness to Canada, it must be pointed out that these insects are not prevalent year-round. The black flies are bad only during a month or so in the middle of the summer. And the mosquitoes, I understand, migrate south for the winter, flapping their huge wings in formation like a flight of mallards. The Canadians spend a lot of time and money on mosquito control; it must be risky business, as I'm sure some of them can only be shot down by Royal Canadian Air Force fighter pilots in grim, hand-to-hand aerial combat.

But as a reflex-action training ground, this area could not be beat. Our kids refused to stay in the rig when all outdoors beckoned to be investigated, and they learned early to cope with the insects. Thanks to developing instantaneous reactions, they could swat a mosquito or black fly while it was still licking its chops in anticipation, and it was nothing to see the house apes, playing outside, all but engulfed in a stack of corpses without receiving so much as a bite. This early indoctrination was to serve them in good stead in later life, when they had to cope with the bloodsuckers from the Infernal Revenue Service.

These same Canadian lakes and rivers that breed the mosquitoes also have a very salutary effect on the reflexes of the oldsters. You see, these watering holes also contain fighting fish that challenge the Izaak Walton in us all—not to mention the hunters who dote on all manner of wild waterfowl.

It's never been established for sure whether sportsmen are attracted to the RV lifestyle, or whether RVers become sportsmen by virtue of spending so much time outdoors. But one thing is certain: The stalkers of salmon, trout, bass, and fighting muskellunge, as well as the hunters of duck, geese, quail, and pheasant, do not fill their frying pans and their Dutch ovens by being sluggish in their reflex reactions. Is it any wonder, then, that the RVer is universally recognized as not only being quick of wit, but lightning of response?

Now lest this be considered a trait dominated by the male species, I hasten to point out that the female RVer is equally adept when it comes to speedy reaction time. For example:

When Dortha goes to the RV fridge, especially after a choppy ride, she automatically assumes a Pete Rose stance with her hands extended, ready to catch whatever is going to fly out. This is a conditioned reflex in response to having been bombarded by all types of things whenever the refrigerator door is opened after a trip of any duration.

I have seen her put a Dodgers' shortstop to shame by the way she can field a flying bottle of catsup with one hand, a tumbling pickle jar with the other, and a butter dish in her teeth. A Yugoslavian juggler would be hard-pressed to emulate her backhand recovery of a milk carton, while juggling an errant cantaloupe and an eggplant.

But what really won her the fielder-of-the-year award was an astonishingly fast reaction time that should be recorded in the *Guinness Book of World Records*. It happened in Chicken, Alaska, after Rocinante had been massaged by a particularly nasty bit of graveled road. I made the mistake of opening the refrigerator in search of a sorely needed beer.

As the door swung open, the fridge gave birth to a chocolate cream pie that sailed out, scooted right across my surprised palms, skidded across the kitchen counter, and soared right out the front door, where it was deftly fielded by the distaff, who dropped her broom just in time to catch the soaring pastry without so much as marring the meringue topping (or inter-rupting her conversation).

Needless to say, my admiration for my distaff—nearly al-ways at peak load—reached on this day a level of unchartered heights. What a woman!

And so, with daily challenges like this, it is little wonder that our great fraternity of RVers have whetstoned their normal re-flex actions to the point where they are the envy of the world. Indeed, the Artful Dodger himself could do no better than a seasoned motorhome pilot when it comes to dodging potholes in the road, compensating for the air pressures of a passing 18-wheeler, or skillfully threading his motorhome through a traffic-choked freeway.

All of which is yet another interesting facet of our great fam-ily of recreational vehicle buffs.

The Merry Widows

Kamloops, British Columbia, a neat little city boasting several nice campgrounds, is noted primarily for being the home of the Kamloops trout—the fightingest, pink-fleshed fish that ever chomped a dry fly.

The wife and I had sprung for a night on the town and were just returning to Rocinante when we noticed an Airstream trailer parked in the stall next to ours. For some reason, for a parked trailer, it seemed to be doing a lot of shaking. It was all lit up, and there was the high peal of female laughter issuing through its open windows.

We readied for bed, and when the din showed no signs of quieting down, the wife decided I should go over and do something about it.

"Live and let live, dear," I said feebly. "Probably a group of nice young ladies running a floating sporting house, peddling their wares door-to-door to henpecked husbands."

"You go over and tell them to quiet down. And to watch their language. It's too hot to close the windows, and we won't be able to sleep a wink."

"Yes, dear." I dutifully clicked off the television, went next door and knocked on the Airstream. As I did so, I noticed a huge pair of mud-encrusted cowboy boots on the step. I was giving serious thought to aborting this mission when the door opened.

"Come in," cooed a feminine voice.

I went in, stooping to accommodate the low doorway, and stood up inside. I fully expected to see a wanton scene of debauchery: flowing booze, empty bottles, the flash of naked flesh.

I saw four elderly women playing canasta.

"Welcome to the MWPP, young fellow," said one of the elderly women, a big-bosomed mother hen. "You married?"

"The name's Anderson. I'm from the motorhome next door. I..."

"Well, sit ye down, neighbor. Have a drink," said a chipper little sparrow, who had obviously witnessed a great many yesterdays. "Or would you rather have a beer?"

"A beer will do very nicely," I said, trying to gather my wits.

"Anything you like. The MWPP strives to please."

"The MWPP?"

"The Merry Widows Peripatetic Parlor." I was handed a beer in a tall pilsener glass.

"I see," I said, not seeing at all. "Is the MWPP some kind of organization?"

"You bet your bustle," said the little sparrow. "It's an organization of four old widowed bats who have decided to see the country instead of sitting home and fossilizing in a rocking chair. Did you say you were married?"

"'Fraid so," I said, unable to suppress a grin.

"Well, you're welcome anyhow. Wanna play a little poker?"

"Thanks a lot, but I'm here on a mission."

"Sit right here next to Agnes," said the sparrow. "And Agnes, you watch your hands. We'll play straight he-man poker. No baseball, spit-in-the-ocean, toilet flush, or any of those bird droppings. Straight stud. OK?"

"OK." I found myself shoved into a seat next to a twinkle-eyed hummingbird.

"And Agnes," said the little sparrow, addressing the hummingbird, "since you're sitting by that nice man, you behave yourself."

"You just tend to your own business, Millicent," said the hummingbird, surveying me through sultrily lowered eyelids.

It turned out to be as lively a poker game as I have ever been involved in, and that includes more than a few poker decks worn thin during my military career. I found out during the time it took me to lose my shirt that the MWPP had a membership of four widows whose families had flown the nest. The widows had all chipped in to buy a small but nice travel trailer and were spending their time seeing the world instead of sitting home molting and being problems to children and inlaws.

They spent the summer in the north and the winter in the south. They liked to fish, gossip, play canasta and poker, and hunt for husbands—not necessarily in that order. They found they could do all these things better and cheaper in their roving aluminum parlor, living grandly off their Social Security checks. In short, they were having a ball.

When the knock came on the door, I knew who it was. The missus had come over to pull her spouse out of the sin sink he had evidently fallen into, and there was blood in her eye. When she saw my septuagenarian partners, however, the daggers in her eyes changed to question marks and finally to merriment as she joined the poker game.

It was 2 A.M. before the game broke up and we were reluctantly escorted to the door. On the way out I tripped over the huge cowboy boots and went sprawling. "Would you kindly tell me," I said, picking myself up, "who belongs to the cowboy boots?"

Agnes laughed. "We bought those at a flea market. When we girls don't want to be bothered, we just put those size 14 boots out on the step. Would you bother anyone in the trailer who'd fit those boots?"

I laughed. "No way. They would have discouraged me. But there's one thing more threatening than a guy who wears size-14 boots."

"What's that?" asked Agnes.

"A redheaded wife who can't sleep."

As I undressed for bed, reeking of kippered herring and Limburger cheese, I couldn't help but chuckle over the evening's activities. "Isn't that something—those old gals traveling around the country?"

"I think it's just marvelous," said the redhead. "It certainly beats living in an old folks' home, or being shunted off, unwanted, into the back room of an in-law's home. But how do you suppose they can afford to flit around the country in a nice Airstream and a new Chrysler?"

"I know how."

"How?"

"By luring unsuspecting men into their roving gambling den and then fleecing them."

Dortha laughed. "Don't knock private enterprise."

"I'm not knocking it. But I always considered myself a fairly handy poker player. That gang of insidious black widows got me for fourteen bucks!"

So we come to the moral of this story, dear readers. If an Airstream trailer with the initials MWPP over the door happens to pull into your campground, make it a point to meet the lovely ladies who inhabit it. But if you should happen to be drawn into one of their poker games—and you will—just remember the old adage:

Never, but never, try to draw to an inside straight.

The Ultimate Test

There are many proving grounds for really testing the integrity of a motorhome. One may bounce over the frost heaves of the Alcan Highway during the spring thaw; one may gallop through the *topes* and *vados* of the Baja Peninsula roads following a heavy rain; or one may simply lock airhorns with a speeding Amtrak train.

Engaging in any of the above pursuits will certainly underscore the weak spots in your rig. There is yet another method, however, much simpler and easier, to truly test the structural engineering of a motorhome.

I refer, of course, to inviting the grandchildren to accompany you on a weekend trip.

Big Red and I have six of the little critters. I suspect that by and large ours are no better or worse than any run-of-the-mill grandget. They come in assorted colors, sizes, shapes, and sexes.

Part of the problem with our set of ankle biters is that their mothers have always let them in the house. It follows that if parents let children into the house, the next thing you know they'll be up at the table. Then, God forbid, in your bed. It's bad enough to have a cat or dog share your eiderdown.

So with this background established, you will understand how a few days with our grandget were to test the mettle of our Rocinante in a manner that would make the Aberdeen Proving Ground look to its laurels.

It all started on a nice summer day when Dortha and I scooped up the grandkids for a weekend of dry camping on a quiet beach near Lincoln, Oregon. At least it started out quiet. Looking back, it all seemed so innocent. . . .

"Andy!" There was no mistaking the sense of urgency in the missus' voice, hailing me from the bathroom.

"Yes, love?"

"Would you turn up the water pressure? The shower's dribbling."

"I don't know how to tell you this, my dove, but it's not pressure we're low on. It's water." My observation was punctuated by a loud gurgling sound, followed by a hissing of air. "See?"

The head that poked out of the bathroom door wore a mask of thick lather. The eyes poking through the lather were not regarding me kindly. "I thought you filled the tanks. You knew we were dry camping."

"True, love. But little Ryan discovered the outside drain and decided to build a swimming pool for his hamster. He did quite a nice job, actually."

"I'm covered head to toe with soapsuds. What are you going to do?"

"I was thinking of bumming a cup of freshly brewed coffee from one of our neighbors."

"Andy Anderson! You do something, and you do it quick! I'm beginning to itch."

Hosing one's distaff down with a six-pack of quinine water is not the best way to start the day. Nor was the redhead's mood elevated when we found Allison had given her pet a bath and decided to dry it off in the microwave. Fortunately the generator was not running, or we'd have redecorated the coach in wall-to-wall gerbil.

The evening brought on the pillow fight, followed by one of the urchins knocking the television off the shelf, which was accompanied by a hellacious boom as the cathode tube imploded. Fortunately, there was no electrical fire, thanks to the fact that the circuits had all blown when Rachel had inserted her weiner toaster into the wall plug.

But things took a definite turn for the worse when Gwendy walked through the screen door without bothering to open it, and we found ourselves in night maneuvers with all types of interesting predatory insects. Along toward morning, when I was fighting for my life with a mosquito the size of a muscular goshawk, had anyone approached with a five-dollar bill, they would have been the instant owner of a motorhome complete with its own demolition squad.

The following morning things were fairly quiet, as I had convinced the cherubs to go out on the beach and play in the undertow. It was just before lunch when Allison made an appearance to announce that one of her goldfish had been ailing, so she had put half a dozen Alka Seltzers into the bowl for instant relief. She now carried around a goldfish bowl with the carcasses of six bellied-up fish whose spirits had just been fizzed into the pearly gates.

Had I been less than an abstemious man, I might have been forced to fortify myself with a wee dollop of the dew following the incident with Serendipity. Serendipity belongs to the grandget and is a mangy mutt of a size that should be more at home in the Kentucky Derby than in a backyard dog house.

"It's Serendipity," announced Allison, giving me a worried look as she squeezed through the hole in the screen door.

"What's the matter with your dog?"

"He won't come home."

"Good," I said, swatting a mosquito that was poised to fly off with my wife.

"It's all because of Fifi," said the moppet, looking up at me through eyes the size of hubcaps.

"Fifi? Who's Fifi?"

"Fifi," said Allison, her large eyes melting with adoration, "is the cutest little French poodle you ever saw."

"Poodle? What in blazes does that splay-gaited fleabag see in a tiny poodle?"

"I think," said Allison, wrinkling her nose in confidence, "Serendipity is in love."

"Whatever it is," said grandson Ryan, "Dippy won't leave. He just whines at the front door of that little camper over there."

"Good Lord!" I said. "I'd better go get him. If that Sherman tank takes a swipe at that camper door, the whole rig will topple over the cliff."

The grandkids were right. Serendipity had fallen in love. Although Fifi was little larger than one of Dippy's ears, this mattered not a mite to the huge mastiff, who took the capriciousness of Mother Nature in stride and launched an amorous campaign of courtship that included such seductive overtures as pawing, drooling, and braying like a gutshot coyote.

Fifi, being a typical female, reposed in aloof dignity on the inside of the camper and contemptuously surveyed the whole frustrating scene through the window. It took the five of us to load the amorous hound into a borrowed wheelbarrow and wheel him, protesting bitterly, back to Rocinante, where he was incarcerated under lock and key. There, much to the wife's vocal laments, he spent the afternoon rocking the rig with guttural growls and swinging thumps of his tail as he tried to bury his bone in the kitchen linoleum.

We lost little time getting under way that evening.

Looking back on the affair, several things were established: First, Rocinante is truly a champion. She had survived the world's toughest proving ground, and except for several cosmetic blemishes, had prevailed like a winner. And second, it's a mathematical fact that six kids are not six times as bad as one kid; they are six to the sixth power as bad. Therefore, never go camping with: six grandkids; six goldfish (dead); assorted hamsters and/or gerbils; or a mutt the size of a moose.

Our motorhome passed the test. As to Grandma and Grandpa, we'll know as soon as the casts have been removed.

Does all this mean we don't love our grandkids? Of course not. In truth, we have six of the cutest little angels who ever stuck a cat's tail in a wall socket. Pardon me while I get my wallet. I just happen to have thirty or forty pictures. . . .

Gabby to the Rescue

There is no stronger bond among perfect strangers than that shared by those who belong to the great fraternal order of RV owners. This common denominator is the badge of courage that immediately identifies one as a kindred soul, a fellow traveler, one who has suffered the slings and arrows of outrageous misfortune. There is no such thing as an independent RV owner. Sooner or later one finds himself in a position where he needs assistance—generally acute.

It all stems from the days of the Wild West, when the pioneers discovered that wagon drivers who banded together stood the best chance of crossing the prairies with scalps intact. As a leftover from the old days, the nomadic wanderer of today, hauling his aluminum wagon, still shares with his fellow travelers a rapport that transcends all levels and knows no class distinction.

This was graphically demonstrated when we recently pulled into a California campground with our new rig. There is nothing like shining, unsullied fiberglass to gain the attention of this great fraternity. Members theorize that the new rig owner is probably a novice and therefore needs all the help that he can get.

Furthermore, the gregarious assemblage that gathers to help the newcomer park is usually divided into two major groups: the Rightists, who think the steering wheel should be turned to the right, and Leftists, who oppose this movement. There are also two smaller splinter groups: the Back-uppers and the Go-forwarders. Each camp has a leader who issues instructions in a very loud and commanding voice.

Rocinante suddenly became as recalcitrant as a balky mule. She became more skittish and nervous with each command, and it was only after I completely ignored the verbal directions that I managed to get her into her stall at all, and then at an embarrassing angle that caused much head-shaking among the spectators. I wanted no more of it. I turned off the ignition.

As I did so, an old-timer with a face wreathed in long white whiskers approached and squeezed a few words by the shank of an old corncob pipe that was obviously rooted to his gums. "That ain't gonna hack it, son."

I studied the face stolen from Gabby Hayes and noted the gums were entirely bereft of teeth. "I'll have you know, sir, that the rig may be new, but the driver is not. I'm an old pro."

"Then why didja park on the wrong side of the outlets?"

I looked back to see that the rig's hookups were on the opposite side of the space's. "Well, whaddaya know."

"Pull her up again," said the corncob owner. "Park on the other side of the pole."

With no little difficulty, I again went through the parking procedure, ignoring everyone but Gabby Hayes. Finally properly stalled, I dismounted and started administering to Rocinante's needs. By the time I had her leveled, Gabby had plugged in the power, the water, and the sewer connection. I pulled a couple of chairs out of the storage compartment and unfolded them.

"Come sundown," I said, "I've been known to have a wee dollop of the dew. Care to join me?"

"Well," said Gabby, easing into a chair, "that might be right neighborly."

I grabbed a bottle of Wild Turkey and a couple of glasses. "The name's Anderson."

"Just call me Gabby," he said, pumping my hand. "Everybody says I look like Gabby Hayes in the movies, so I don't fight it none. Besides, it's kinda fun signin' autographs. Nobody seems to mind that Gabby's been dead for years."

"What kind of mix would you like with your booze?"

"Mix? You loco, pardner? That's sippin' whiskey. Don't never do nothin' to sippin' whiskey but sip it." He put the bottle to his lips and took a three-gulp sip. "Lawze, that's fine booze!" He handed me the bottle and wiped his mouth with his sleeve.

To be sociable, I took a large sip. "You sure seem to know your RVs," I said. "Bet you're an old prospector and used to live in one."

"Done a little prospectin'. No money in it, though. Turned to runnin' a chuck wagon."

"A chuck wagon?"

"A travel trailer decked out as a chuck wagon. Pulled it behind my Jeep. Down in Texas. Did right well, too, for an uneducated man."

" Somehow," I said, taking another sip, "that's a field of endeavor I never figured was very lucrative."

"Drivin' a chuck wagon?" Gabby reached for the bottle. "Hell, yes. Guess I worked the whole panhandle of Texas at one time or another before I retired."

"With the big cattle ranches?"

"Cattle ranches?" He looked at me with disgust. "What's cattle ranches got to do with it?"

"Sheep ranches?"

"Hell, I didn't work no ranches. No money in that. I used to drive my chuck wagon from the wet counties to the dry ones.

Hauled moonshine. Could carry fifty gallons in my trailer's water tank. Know what booze sells for in a dry Texas county?"

"Yes," I said, remembering my old flying-cadet days in San Antonio. "Plenty."

"Never did get caught—even suspicioned. Who'd ever think of lookin' for booze in a chuck wagon? Made enough to retire and buy me a little rig. Now I just foller the sun."

"That's a fascinating story."

"Ain't it. Well, it's been fun jawbonin', but I'd better get back to my own digs. Just have time for a short one before Gunsmoke comes on."

"How about one for the road?" I asked, handing him the bottle.

"Maybe just a little sip for the ditch." He took another little sip that all but drained the bottle. "Good luck to you, neighbor."

"Good luck to you, Gabby." I shook his hand. "And thanks for your help."

"Weren't nothin'."

I watched him weave through several RV lots toward an ancient trailer with a rack of prospecting tools on the roof. He reached the old trailer and then, to my surprise, turned right, went down two more lots, and entered the largest Airstream in the park. Complete with air-conditioners and a rear-mounted satellite dish, it beggared quarters usually associated with the Hilton hotel chain. And it was obvious that Gabby had no trouble pulling his huge rig, for the beefy Chevy pickup parked alongside provided more than enough horsepower.

I chuckled to myself. Once again I had been smitten by my favorite attraction of this unfolding RV drama: its fantastic cast of characters.

I took the last swig from the bottle and chased it with a large inhalation of aromatic spaghetti sauce emanating from Dortha's kitchen. Suddenly my attention was commanded by a comely young lady with a size 36 brisket, wearing a size 24 bikini top, who was hanging up clothes in the lot next door.

This RV life could, I ruminated, be downright addictive if not approached very, very carefully.

Really Roughing It

Big Red and I think that state campgrounds are nifty because they've got lots of trees. And trees are nifty 'cause when you find a couple close together you can hang a hammock between them. And hammocks are nifty 'cause you can lie in one with a good book and a jar of grape squeezings and toast the sunset in regal splendor while watching the spouse wash the motorhome.

Recently in one of our favorite campgrounds I was thus employed, happily hammocking away, when my reverie was shattered by the low growl of a diesel that could only have come from an Amtrak locomotive. Half expecting to see the Sunset Limited chugging through, I laid down my book to see a sight equally as disturbing. A motorhome roughly the size of Shea Stadium was backing into the campsite next door.

The maneuver was being beautifully orchestrated by a healthy young damsel wearing a black leather outfit that could only have been donned with a shoehorn. Standing in front of the video camera that commanded the rear of the rig, she skillfully guided the driver into the spot, using body language one seldom associates with the plugging in of a motorhome.

With the rig precisely positioned, she slid her forefinger across her throat and the driver dutifully chopped the engine. She spotted me, gave a friendly wave, then skipped around the coach to disappear inside. A whirring noise punctured the silence, then levelers extended from the rig's nether regions to level the motorhome fore and aft. This was followed by a pneumatic thump as room extenders began blossoming from both sides of the unit. It quickly assumed dimensions that could easily hangar a dirigible.

Another whirring noise issued from the roof, where a satellite dish was rising like a phoenix from the ashes. The automatic satellite-seeking system made several bracketing maneuvers, then locked on to the orbiting satellite that would provide crystal-clear reception to the televisions below.

As I watched in bemusement, a very large man dismounted, then walked slowly around the rig, checking things out. Spotting me, he came over to my hammock and introduced himself. "Hi, neighbor." My hand was gripped in a heavy-duty vise disguised as a fist. "Name's Harry Throckmorton."

With some difficulty I extracted myself from the hammock, retrieved my mangled fingers, and said, "Andy Anderson. Nice to know you."

"Nice spot you got here, Andy."

"Thank you. We like it." I noticed he was wearing a bulky survival vest, not unlike the type worn by jet pilots in combat. "It's none of my business, Harry, but wouldn't it have been easier to plug in your sewer hose before extending your slide-outs?"

"Sewer hose?" He chuckled. "You're living in the dark ages, Andy. This rig is equipped with the state-of-the-art Incinolet."

"Incinolet? I don't believe I'm familiar with. . . ."

"Greatest RV john ever invented. No germs or liquids to worry about. Uses toilet-bowl liners. After heeding nature's nudge, you push a button. The paper liner and waste drop into a chamber where the works are zapped with a heating element that incinerates everything. You just empty the ashes every week or so. No smell, no muss, no fuss."

"But how about gray water? Surely . . ."

"Gray water's nothing but soapsuds. Soap's made out of the same ingredients as fertilizer. I just find a spot that needs to be fertilized and let fly. Environmentalists love me."

"But with all those electrical gadgets, don't you use an awful lot of juice?"

"Yep. I'm an engineer. Designed this rig myself. See my roof? One huge solar panel. And I carry more batteries than a submarine. Have a nice 10-kw generator I crank up when Minerva uses the treadmill. That's what she's doing now."

"You have a treadmill? When you have this beautiful forest campground to hike around in?"

"Minerva likes to use the treadmill. Then she can pop right into the sauna when she's finished exercising."

"The sauna. You have a sauna in your rig?"

"Of course. Don't you?"

I looked over at poor old Rocinante, being groomed by the distaff. She looked so forlorn by comparison, I fought the urge to go over and hug her. "In our rig we're lucky to have indoor plumbing."

"We replaced the Jacuzzi with the sauna. That way, we have more room for the wine cellar."

"That makes sense." As we talked Harry produced an object from a pocket of his survival vest and started fiddling with it.

"May I ask what you have there?"

"It's a Garmin GPS. Best personal navigator on the market. I'm turning it on," he said.

"GPS? I seem to have trouble keeping up with this conversation."

"Global Positioning System. Works off the satellites. It will pinpoint your exact position at all times. See this display? Shows where the satellites are. I punch this button and it locks in the exact latitude and longitude location of our home base. Would you like to know your coordinates?"

"Not especially, no."

"I wouldn't go hunting or fishing without a GPS. You can't get lost with this little beauty. Just push this button, and no matter where you are, it shows you the direction and the distance back to your home base."

"Dandy."

"Remember Captain O'Grady, the pilot who punched out over Bosnia? He had a GPS receiver that enabled the rescue crews to pinpoint his location. If it weren't for one of these little babies, O'Grady would still be munching bugs."

"I'll have to get one for Big Red. She gets lost a lot."

As I watched, the big man stuffed the GPS receiver back into one pocket of his survival vest and produced another small computer. "It's time to think about putting on the feed bag." He started punching the computer's buttons.

"What have we here?" I asked.

"This is the new handy-dandy Road Whiz Ultra. It shows all you need to know about interstate travel." He read the display printout. "Good. We have a pizza parlor three miles down the road. I'll call their number." He pulled a cellular phone from yet another pocket and started dialing. "You and your lady are joining us for an impromptu dinner."

"I'll have to check with the redhead. . . ."

He placed a pizza order and hung up. "Dinner will be here in half an hour. Just time for a small libation." As if on cue, Minerva approached from the rig bearing four glasses of champagne and a tray of canapes. "I'm partial to Dom Perignon's 1987 vines, aren't you, Andy?"

"Never drink anything else but."

"Goes well with a bit of caviar. I like my beluga chilled at forty degrees. I hope this is to your liking." As I took a canape, Throckmorton took a big swig from his glass, swallowed, smacked his lips, then inhaled deeply.

"By God, smell that fresh, clean air." He turned to me. "Ain't it great getting out here with Mother Nature and really roughing it?"

"Yep," I said, taking a large swallow of Dom Perignon, "there's nothing quite like getting out here with Mother Nature and really roughing it."

Leave the Driving to Them

Do you occasionally suffer from freeway frazzle? Are you tired of potholes turning your beautiful RV into the world's largest salad tosser? Are you about ready to put out a contract on the next truck driver that tries to blow you off the road with his airhorn? Do you find you have to pry white knuckles off the steering wheel just from driving your rig into a gas station?

Then release that pedal from the metal, fellow vagabond, for have we got a deal for you.

Sometimes we get so caught up in today's pressurized rat race, with the low-tech highways and high-tech ulcers, that we forget why it was that we bought an RV in the first place. Sometimes we forget that if we don't stop to sniff the roses once in a while, we may forget what it feels like to inhale a bumblebee. Not to mention how badly a cardiac arrest can screw up an afternoon of golf.

Fortunately, there are many ways in which the locomotion of one's RV may be delegated to someone outside of the cockpit, leaving the RV captain free to engage in less onerous pursuits, such as smooching with one's copilot or contemplating one's navel—something we seldom seem to find enough time for these days.

Our favorite surrogate driver is a Mexican engineer who has no teeth, but beautiful gums. Jose runs the Mexican locomotive that pulls the freight cars upon which a group of us recently parked our RVs for a trip through Mexico's Copper Canyon.

Mexico's Sierra Madres have always held a certain fascination, but only one road crosses this remote region, a pixilated iron highway called the Chihuahua Al Pacifico, which soars from sea level to 8,000 feet across the backbone of the Continental Divide.

We had always heard that unless one is taking chickens to market, Mexican railroads have all the allure of a tax audit. Their reputation has long been a deterrent to seeing this fascinating country. But now it was possible to see it all from the comfort of one's own RV—while leaving the driving to José. Or so the brochure said. What would it really be like to strap one's rig to a flatcar and spend five nights on a Mexican freight train? Curiosity overcoming trepidation, we had to find out.

And we did. The trip was marvelous. Nothing could compare with taking in the rugged splendor of Mexico's Grand Canyon from the armchair of a living room on wheels. In spite of freezing weather, blizzards, and train derailments, this laid-back, piggyback trip on the Chihuahua Al Pacifico Railroad was truly an unforgettable experience. And with José doing the driving, there wasn't a white knuckle in the crowd.

Okay, so Mexican freight trains don't toot your whistle. How about driving your rig onto a river barge? Flat-bottom boats now come complete with all hookups and offer you the choice of several venues. You may cruise the Mississippi and leave the driving to Captain Andy, your friendly tugboat captain. While you lower your awning, trot out your camp chairs, and nurse a mint julep, Captain Andy will thread your barge through the locks of Mighty Ole Miss.

Viewing the Hiawatha country of Minnesota, the Mississippi river haunts of Huck Finn, the battle sites of the Civil

War, the antebellum homes of the Deep South—there is nothing quite like a trip on our nation's main artery for lovers of our history, beauty, and culture.

Or, if you prefer, Captain François will do the same on his tugboat, tooting your barge through the fascinating backwater bayous of Louisiana.

For our RVers who want to visit Alaska but are skittish about scrubbing their bottoms on the washboard highways, the excellent ferries of the Alaskan system can be boarded with one's RV. Although one cannot live in one's rig on the ferryboats, clean accommodations are provided on the ship, and watching the gorgeous scenery float by while nestled in a deck chair sure beats worrying about flat tires, frayed tempers, and windshield dings.

The ultimate RV is still in the prototype stage, but it promises to be the panacea for highway hangups. The RV is shaped like a large gondola, about the same size and dimensions of a nice-sized travel trailer. This gondola fits neatly under the rotor blades of a large helicopter. Whenever RVers living in the gondola wish a change of venue, they just contact the chopper pilot. He swoops down, latches on to their rig, and whisks it off to the new desired location.

By leaving the driving to Captain Future, one may really relax and enjoy the ride—providing the checklist is dutifully followed and all of the ganglia properly disconnected before flight. A deviation from this policy might well engender friction with one's neighbors, especially if they see a sewer hose swinging overhead.

Good Sam's excellent tour office can help make arrangements for much of the foregoing (888) 893-4629, or can put you in touch with those who do.

So the next time you get the urban uptights, the highway hives or the traffic trauma—take a little time off. Take advantage of one of the many opportunities now available for leaving the driving to someone else for a change of pace. Whether turning over the throttle to Engineer José or Captains Andy, Francis, or Future, this can have a most salubrious effect on one's outlook and enjoyment of the RV lifestyle.

Not to mention the savings on gasoline, tires, vehicle maintenance, and antacid pills. And who knows? It might even improve your love life.

Mangoes, Mariachis, and Montezuma's Revenge

It was in Chihuahua, Mexico, many years ago. The little tyke, barely four feet tall in his thick-soled sandalias, wore a serape and a sombrero nearly as big as he was. He looked up at me with dancing eyes the size of tortillas and whispered in hushed tones as he pulled an object from the folds of his serape.

"*Pssst, señor.* You want to buy the skull of Pancho Villa? A very good price."

I looked curiously at the object in his hand. It was a small skull, probably that of a monkey. "*Muchacho*, I always thought Pancho Villa was a big man."

"*Si, señor.* He was beeg. But this is the skull of Pancho Villa when he was a leetle boy."

It was hard to refute this logic. I emerged from this strange encounter with not only the skull of Pancho Villa when he was a leetle boy, but an everlasting love for Mexico and its people.

Happily, Big Red shares this romance, and over the years the bride and I have journeyed far and wide within its borders. We have plugged our sewer hose into most of the main cities, including its jewel, Mexico City, one of the most cosmopolitan cites in the world and one of the few that has been declared a national historic monument.

One has not seen Mexico until one has seen Mexico City. To sweep down its magnificent aorta, the Paseo de la Reforma is to journey through time while holding hands with Cortés and Montezuma.

Another favorite used to be Guadalajara. At one time, we actually considered retirement at nearby Lake Chapala, where thousands of Americans have settled. At that time, one could buy a small furnished house for less than $10,000 right on the lake. But we found our U. S. ties too strong to break so we never took up residence in Mexico. If one caters to a large metropolitan area of 3.5 million souls, however, Guadalajara is still a nice place to visit.

Another ingratiating locale is San Miguel De Allende. This color-postcard city, which clings to the side of a mountain, is a mecca for art students from all the Americas. RVers Dan and Muriel Phippen from Tempe, Arizona, have often journeyed to this historic setting, staying for months at a time while living with a Mexican family to polish up their conversational Spanish.

The city of Taxco has always appealed to the history buff in Dortha, it being the oldest mining town in North America. Taxco is scattered over a rugged hillside in the heart of the Sierra Madres; the bell in the tower of the ancient Santa Prisca church echoes throughout this fascinating national monument that has changed little since the days when Cortés's captains discovered rich gold deposits in its environs.

Our favorite place to shop in all Mexico is "Lucky Pucky," as Americans call it. Tlaquepaque is a picturesque suburb of Guadalajara, and not only is it recognized as the origin of the mariachi stroller, but its factories of glass, silverware, copperware, leather goods, furniture, and sculpture are known throughout Mexico. Many of its factory stores are open to the public and are fascinating.

However, it has always been the Mexico back roads that kept calling us back to Mexico. Years ago, when we first learned about the magnificent Mexican Copper Canyon (the *Barranca del Cobra*), and how it was an RV trip you literally had to train for, Dortha and I couldn't wait to herd our rig onto a Mexican square-wheeled flatcar. Subscripting a dozen buddies, all of us muscled our RVs onto the freight cars in Chihuahua and spent five days clickety-clacking along the old railroad track that meandered through the Sierra Madres like a pixilated garter snake, leaving the driving to José Gonzales.

At that time, it was the only way to view captivating Copper Canyon, reputed to be four times as large as our Grand Canyon, and it turned out to be one of the greater RVing adventures of our lifetime. Until one has had a snowball fight and shared a cerveza with a Tarahumara Indian in his cave, one has not truly lived.

And if one is a refugee from the rat race, one would be hard-pressed to get away from it all any farther than a visit to the unique village of Creel, the midway point on the Chihuahua-Pacifico Railway that traverses the Copper Canyon. With its nearly 8,000-foot altitude and its tiny population of loggers, its chances of being spoiled by the Mexico tourist explosion are quite remote.

We love the coastal towns of Guaymas, Los Mochis, and Culiacán—pearls in a string of small towns strung along Mexico's west coast— where the fishing and shopping are superb, and the small-town ambience has been preserved. Mazatlán is becoming a little too commercialized and too touristy for our druthers, threatening to become another Acapulco. However, Mazatlán is a good jumping off spot for La Paz, Baja California Sur, if one deigns to throw caution to the winds and take a Mexican ferryboat.

There is something about seeing your little home-away-from-home being swallowed up by the maw of a Mexican ocean thrasher, and a trip across the Gulf of California can rank right up there with adventure of the highest order. Caution: Attempting this trip without knowing the Mexican word for seasick pills could be hazardous to your health. A trip through the Baja California Peninsula is what an RV is designed for. Its scenic towns, stunning sunsets, and remote beaches are guaranteed to unknot the uptights. Cabo San Lucas, a former cannery village on its southern tip, alone is worth the visit. For the worm-drowners among us, there is no better sport fishing on this planet: sailfish, marlin, and smaller game fish leap to the lure all year long.

The only problem, as with so many other beautiful resorts in Mexico, is that this picturesque former pirate's hideout is becoming swamped by luxury hotels, condominiums, restaurants, and boutiques that seriously test the resolve of its natives to maintain its charm and long-established ways.

Where we used to park our motorhome on the sandy beach to watch the ocean swirl through the pinnacle rocks and the natural arches, there now stands a high-rise. And private yachts have replaced old pirate ships in the harbor.

There is no doubt about it. Mexico is outgrowing its sombrero and its mañana lala-land attitude. Americans, Canadians, and other foreigners are flocking in droves to its resort towns to sop up its balmy climate, its beauty, its cheap economy. And this laid-back country and its people are going through a traumatic change. The jury is still out debating the effectiveness of NAFTA, and the country has recently been torn by revolutions, political assassinations, and devaluation of the peso.

Just how is Mexico coping with all these changes? The time had come to revisit this popular destination; time to get an update on how our neighbors to the south are faring today. Is it still a good, safe, economical place to visit? Are gringos and their RVs still welcome guests?

The copilot and I just completed a trip to Mexico to find out. We'll answer these questions in the next chapter by reporting on a sojourn to one of our favorite spots, one of the best-kept secrets in all Mexico. So, stay tuned. Or, as we say in Mexico, "*Hasta lumbago.*"

Mangoes, Mariachis, and Montezuma's Revenge (Parté Dos)

In the previous chapter we extolled the virtues of the old Mexico that had been our RV playground for some three decades. Since that time, this colorful country and its people have been wracked by change; assassinations, political upheaval, NAFTA, and the devaluation of the peso have created a Latin pressure cooker that sorely threatens its safety valve.

What effect has all this had on a country that is fast becoming one of the more popular vacation destinations? Has the influx of foreigners from the United States, Canada, and Europe served to strip Mexico of its charm? To find the answers to these questions, we recently journeyed south of the border to one of our favorite and best-kept secrets in Mexico.

To put this all in proper perspective, a bit of background is in order. One of the advantages of being a poor, impoverished writer is that occasionally one can con one's literary agent into buying lunch. Just such an occasion was transpiring on this day some thirty years ago at a small Hollywood eatery.

As we were slurping our vichyssoise, my agent produced a large map and started unfolding it. "Anderson, you have a few

royalties coming. Here's where I want you to invest them."
He pointed to a small dot on the west coast of Mexico.
I looked at the map. "I don't see anything but a little fishing village."

"Of course you don't. But you will. Ava Gardner and Dick Burton have just finished making a movie there. A turkey called *Night of the Iguana*. It's going to put Puerto Vallarta on the map. A few of us gringos are tossing some money into the pot to build a nice hotel there. You can get in on the ground floor. Interested?"

"Interested?" I looked at him askance. "That has got to be the most stupid idea I have ever heard. Definitely not! No way! Never! Not on your nachos!"

Fast forward some thirty years. The child bride and I are now shouldering our way through the quarter of a million sun-worshippers that flock like lemmings to Puerto Vallarta in the wintertime—filling to capacity the dozens of spectacular high-rise hotels that anchor its beautiful beaches. Cruise ships further swell the population, disgorging tons of passengers to scuff along its cobblestones in search of elusive bargains. If one looks closely when passing the flea market, one can spot the statue of Liz and Dick, whimsically wondering what has happened to their idyllic fishing village.

Although Puerto Vallarta has many attractions, particularly to the younger crowd who like to barbecue their epidermis in the tropical sun, parasail, and disco 'til dawn—the cultural shock was too much for us, and we lost little time in heading north on Highway 200 to seek climes far less cacophonic.

About fifty miles north of Puerto Vallarta is what used to be the best-kept secret in all Mexico. It's a stunningly beautiful cove called Rincon de Guayabitos. Its adjacent neighbor is a village named La Penita, where cobblestones still echo the hooves of Spanish conquistadors and bloodthirsty pirates. On their silver beaches the fishermen still ply their trade; the shrimp boats bob offshore seining the delicious crustaceans. These are beaches where the Mexicans actually outnumber the gringos.

We were delighted to find the cove has yet to surrender its charm to commercialism, but it's no longer our best-kept secret. A dozen RV parks now dot the beaches, and a couple of nice hotels have been erected. However, if one opts for virginal, solitary shores with nary so much as a TV antenna, nearby are San Francisco Beach, where it's easy to leave your heart, and Lo de Marcos, its curving vista of silver sand backdropped by lush mango trees and coconut palms.

We found there are still beautiful, unsullied vacation spots in Mexico. And if one learns a few words of Spanish and makes a stab at conversation, the Mexican people open up like bougainvillea blossoms. Even our fractured "Spanglish" melted the glass wall between visitors and visitees, and we were welcomed with open arms.

As for prices being cheaper? The peso downslide has not seemed to have much effect on tourist shopping, as most items are pegged to the U.S. dollar. Out of the tourist areas, however, we found great bargains in local restaurants and *supermercados* (supermarkets). Big Red raided a fruit stand and ended up with two huge papayas, a watermelon, a pineapple, a cluster of finger bananas, and a drink of fresh milk right out of the coconut for $2.75.

We ate at one of the best restaurants in La Penita and paid $8 for a delicious langosta (lobster) dinner complete with all the trimmings, margueritas, and tip. The seafood is so fresh it keeps biting your napkin.

Full hookups right on the beach run around $11 per night, including launching ramps for your boat. During their runs, it takes a baseball bat to keep dorado, bonito, and mahi-mahi out of your skiff. Truly an angler's Valhalla. In fact, one of the more popular RV parks is called the Paradiso del Pescador (Fisherman's Paradise).

In talking to a few of the park residents, it was quickly obvious that the park was a fascinating cross-culture of nationalities. Oiling his fishing reel, Vince Oliva was a transplant from Montevideo, Uruguay. He was lamenting the fact that he hadn't been able to catch a bonito weighing over thirty pounds. To him, this slice of Mexico was truly elysium.

Doreen Dassylva from Sonora Island, British Columbia, and Mary Jane Murphy from Toledo, Ohio, were huddled under their palapa playing a card game titled "Murder and Mayhem" that had been going on for the six years they had been bringing their husbands to Mexico. They had observed little change in the Mexican attitude toward foreigners in recent years, finding them to still be warm and friendly. Living was very inexpensive in the Rincon area.

I approached a man launching his fishing boat and made the mistake of mentioning to François LeBlanc from Lyon, France, that I was doing a piece on the Rincon. He all but threatened me with bodily harm for publicizing "the slice of this planet that has no peer in all of Europe, Asia, or the Americas. We must keep thees our secret."

So what did we find on our trip? Our best-kept secret was no longer secret, but Rincon de Guayabitos is still a marvelous place to spend a couple weeks of wintertime. In the back areas prices are cheap, the living is easy, and the pineapples grow tall.

As for security, most everyone we talked to felt every bit as safe in Mexico as they did at home, if not safer. Driving the Mexican roads has not materially improved. All Mexican bus drivers are descendants of Mario Andretti, but if one uses caution, gives the buses and trucks a wide berth, and stays off the highways at night, the roads are little worse than some of our U.S. highways.

The road service monitored by the *Angeles Verdes* (Green Angels) has definitely improved. These green-suited Good Samaritans in their green pickups are truly heaven-sent, rendering free assistance to the RV traveler in trouble. And wonder of wonders, we actually encountered clean rest rooms in some of the Pemex stations. Something unheard of in days of yore.

Bottom line: Should one plan a trip to Mexico in light of current problems? By all means, yes. Common sense must be exercised. Do not park in isolated areas or camp along the highway or on beaches. However, there are marvelous campgrounds throughout Mexico, which are perfectly safe. Gasoline and propane are plentiful. New toll roads are popping up all over the place. In short, proper planning and use of the *Trailer Life Campground/RV Park & Services Directory* can assure a very pleasant vacation.

And if one deigns to really put the blush on the rose, consider one of the organized tours available, and leave all the worries to Wilbur the Wagonmaster. The Good Sam Club has some crackerjack Mexican safaris.

So, in spite of its many problems, Mexico is truly trying to put its best foot forward. After all, tourist dollars are one of its most important revenues. So grab your sombrero, your bean dip, and your suntan lotion and head for Rincon de Guayabitos.

Just don't let some shifty little muchacho try to con you into buying the small skull of Pancho Villa when he was a leettle boy.

I already own it.

Heading North—Maybe

The memsahib snapped her big green eyes at me. "You what?"

"I merely said," I said clearing my throat, "that I've always wanted to see Alaska."

"That isn't all you merely said." She came closer, waving a bread knife uncomfortably close to my Adam's apple. I made a mental note to quit bringing up new ideas in the kitchen.

"Haven't you always wanted to see Alaska?" I said. "Home of the tallest mountain in the United States? Fantastic fishing and—"

"Mosquitoes!" I was happy to see she was attacking a piece of toast rather than my epiglottis. "Mosquitoes that can be picked up on radar."

"Alaska is the last frontier, land of the midnight sun. Where you can still pan for gold and—"

"Freeze to death! Listen, roommate, I'm reaching the age when I want to live in a cozy climate of about 120 degrees. I do not want to be associated with any community where they make houses out of large ice cubes."

"My love! Am I to understand that the spirit of adventure, the lust for new horizons, the itch for new surroundings no longer demands to be scratched?"

"If you want to scratch my itch for new surroundings, how about a Caribbean cruise? Or we could really go adventuring and rough it on the *QE2*. Forget Alaska."

"How can you forget Alaska? It's even bigger than Texas. It's got the Red Dog Saloon. It's the home of Robert W. Service. It's the last bastion of men who draw from the hip and—"

"Forget it, Renfrew of the Mounted." She shoved a dish at me. "And eat your prunes."

A lesser man would have accepted defeat, cashed in his T-bills, and booked passage on the next cruise ship to the Greek Islands for his annual vacation. But not a gent who has memorized "The Cremation of Sam McGee." I would see Alaska, and I would take my roommate with me. Not only is Dortha a good sport, but she would be great company on those Alaskan nights. And with her occasional hot flashes, she could be very warm in bed.

My win-over campaign was a masterpiece of subliminal subtlety. A little bon mot dropped casually into a conversation; a little aside over an hors d'oeuvre; the inviting over for cocktails of a couple friends from Valdez, whom I had prepped not to discuss the oil spill.

Eventually my insidious seduction began to bear fruit. My frequent references to Alaska were met with increasing interest rather than stony indifference, and I felt the time was ripe to administer the coup de grace.

"Do you know," I ventured, "that they now have a luxury liner that carries RVs up the Inside Passage to Skagway and Juneau?"

"A luxury liner?"

"Just like the Love Boat. Only it carries RVs."

"Hold it, roomie. Who said anything about RVs?"

"I think that would be the way to really see Alaska. Carry our own motel. Stay in the beautiful parks. See the splendors of our largest state from the grass roots."

"You mean take an RV to Alaska? With those roads I've heard so much about?"

"People are doing it all the time. I'll be able to fulfill a lifelong ambition. We'll go by boat through the inland waterways and come back on the Alaskan Highway."

"The Alaskan Highway? You mean the famous Alcan that was built during World War II?"

"The same."

"But I've heard such horrible stories about that road!"

"So have I. It's been called the quagmire, the axle-buster, the trail designed by a pugnacious python. Depends on whom you talk to. Some say it's great. Others say it's a washboard nightmare. But I do know that most of it is now paved, and I'd like to find out for myself what it's really like."

She studied my face for a moment, her brows gathered in thought. "This boat—that's like the Love Boat that carries RVs—any shops on board?"

"Nice shops. Duty-free. Great buys on gifts and perfume. And gourmet food served five times a day, several nightclubs, dancing, floor shows, half a dozen bars—"

"Duty-free shops. Maybe we should look into it."

"I already have, love. It seems to be a great way to see parts of Alaska and Canada. In fact, I have the prices right here. Now, the way I see it. . . ." I had touched the right nerve. My wife would take an ice floe to the Galapagos Islands if there were shops on board. I found that my adversary had suddenly turned into a willing accomplice. She not only agreed to accompany me to Alaska, but it took little convincing that we should take an RV, especially since it meant having her own bathroom.

Heeding the advice of old sourdoughs who had made the trek up north, I bought a new 24-foot Class A motorhome. It turned out to be a good choice: big enough for creature comforts, yet nimble and small enough to fit easily onto the boats, ferries, and railroad flatcars we were to encounter.

Now properly outfitted with spare parts, insured, curried, combed, waxed and provisioned, the rig was duly christened Rocinante Two.

D-Day finally arrived. It was a beautiful, windless day, and Rocinante was feeling her oats, pawing at her chocks. Dortha ticked off her closing-the-house checklist, we waved good-bye to neighbors who had come to see us off, I gave Rocinante the spurs, and off we galloped.

We made nearly a block before the CB antenna fell off. It had been glued to the windshield with some type of adhesive that had failed to take its job seriously, and seeing it fall, I slammed on the brakes to keep from running over it. The sudden deceleration upended a poorly stowed container of orange juice in the fridge, and a springlet of juice began cascading onto the floor.

This we noted after we were again under way, and I had stopped after a couple more blocks to check a noise issuing from the left front wheel. While Dortha mopped up orange juice, I drove slowly with my head out the door. Finally divining the noise coming from a loose hubcap, I tightened the protesting wheel cover, and the squeak diminished.

Once more, we started out. This time we made nearly two blocks before gremlins struck again. In taking a rather steep dip in the road, a horrible grating sound emanated from the rear of the coach. I stopped again to investigate and noted the muffler had dragged as the tail end had dipped. Had we overloaded? I elected to call the dealer to ask his advice. In checking for his business card in my wallet, I discovered my billfold was missing. Cursing, I turned Rocinante around and looked back at the distaff, who was squeezing orange juice into the sink.

"I forgot my wallet," I said. "Gotta go back."

"That's good," she said. "I'll pick up some more rags. I think we're going to need them."

"An auspicious beginning. The CB antenna falls off, we baptize the reefer with orange juice, we got a squeaky front end, a dragging rear end, and I forgot my wallet. Here we are, heading for the last frontier and the worst highway ever designed by the hand of man, and we've had five calamities so far, and we're not even a mile from home. Gonna be an interesting trip."

Dortha looked at me and grinned. "Other than that, Mrs. Lincoln, how did you enjoy the play?"

The Stardancer

Part of our grand design of seeing Alaska by motorhome was to heed the message of old Alaskan sourdoughs who fervently claimed that traversing the Alcan Highway one time was interesting, but to do it twice showed the traveler had a large chink in his igloo. For this reason, we had elected to take the luxury liner that carries RVs up the Inside Passage, then return by driving the Alaskan Highway home—only one way.

The sparkling, handsome *Stardancer* was warped up to the Vancouver dock, its stern now a gigantic open maw that was preparing to swallow our RV. It was a prepossessing ship, a marvel of engineering in gleaming white paint, its logo of sun and sea emblazoned on its single smokestack.

Although we were not scheduled to board until 2:30 P.M., by 10 o'clock in the morning a long queue of RVs had started to form. Once the rig was established in line, portable chairs, coffee, and rolls were trotted out in an instant tailgate kaffeeklatsch. No one was about to miss this boat.

Promptly at boarding time, the long line of RVs started to trundle aboard. Efficient deckhands fed us down the ramp and into the bowels of the gleaming ship, Rocinante calm under the spurs, not even dragging her tail on the steep ramp. So efficiently had the German shipbuilders laid out the huge floating garage, there were 110-volt plug-ins every thirty feet. We had no sooner nuzzled Rocinante up to the rear end of the cabover camper in front of us than a deckhand threw us an electrical cord and plugged us in. This was a definite boon, as the propane had to be turned off before boarding the ship, and without being able to switch refrigerators to electricity, many of the well-stocked fridges would have turned into Limburger-cheese lockers by the end of the journey.

Another plus for RVers: Pets could be brought aboard in the rigs. People were allowed below decks to visit their vehicles and tend to their charges, which proved to be a mixed blessing. Arrangements had been made to properly dispose of pet poop, but there are always those who neglect to clean up after their pets, and about the third day we were all candidates for the Bolshoi Ballet, as walking around the hold certainly kept one on one's toes. Rumor has it that the captain inspected the garage on his rounds one day, stepped in a pile, and almost executed a ten-point swan dive into the briny. Needless to say, daily hosing down of the hold was promptly instituted.

Our rigs secured, plugged in, and locked up, we proceeded to the elevator that would take us to our assigned cabin deck. The huge garage was a plush operation indeed. Now we were about to find out whether the *Stardancer* was truly a luxury ship as advertised, or just a glorified ferryboat. If it lived up to its expectations, it would be a miracle, for the price on the *Stardancer*—all things considered—compared very favorably to the tolls of the Alaska Marine Highway ferries that ply the same route. And the latter, although clean and reliable, are somewhat spartan in their eating and sleeping accommodations.

As we alighted in the foyer, stumbling around looking for our cabin, we were amazed at the beauty of the ship. With the aid of willing crew members, we finally found our niche and, opening the door, we were again impressed. The room, if not exactly commodious, was well planned, nicely decorated, and made efficient use of every inch of space. Due to Dortha's claustrophobia, we had sprung for an outside cabin (highly recommended), and the huge porthole not only gave vent to her cooped-up feelings, but provided a beautiful view of the Inside Passage when we glided through.

There was ample closet space, along with a stereo, a telephone, a television, a freshwater shower and sink, and a fascinating, newly designed vacuum-type toilet that promptly became the conversation piece of the ship. Instead of just flushing like any self-respecting commode, it set up sort of a wind-tunnel howl when activated and threatened to suck up everything that wasn't tied down. My wife lost a couple of hair curlers, imprudently stowed on the sink, when she accidentally flushed the john, and it is said that one passenger lost his toupee, literally snatched from his head while he was heeding nature's call.

These picayune problems aside, however, the *Stardancer* cannot be held guilty of false advertising. It proved to have all the amenities of a luxury liner, including a beautiful dining room, a pub bar with live music, the Starlight Nightclub featuring variety shows, the Sundown Lounge for dancing to a good band, a disco, teen and kids' clubs, a health club and spa, a pool with a convertible top to accommodate the weather, numerous bars, a casino, saunas, a hospital, a sport deck, and—naturally—bingo games and lectures. All this and a double-deck garage that could handle 350 vehicles! This one-of-a-kind ship could have been put together only by the man who conceived the famous *Loveboat* of Princess Cruises fame—and it was.

The food turned out to be fabulous, and it was a good thing we were to off-load after three nights, for we rapidly assumed dimensions that were far more porcine than petite. Only the variety shows would leave something to be desired, slightly reminiscent of *The Gong Show*, and the casino slots were deemed a bit uncharitable. Other than that, it was a first-class act all the way.

At 5 P.M. we departed Vancouver, noting in the process what a pretty city it is. We kicked ourselves for not arriving at least a day early to really sightsee this World's Fair locale.

And then, we were slipping past Stanley Park and under Lions Gate Bridge to begin our great North Country odyssey. As we watched Vancouver's beautiful skyline disappear in the wake of the *Stardancer*, we couldn't help but wonder what strange adventures awaited us and Rocinante, our six-wheeled steed, in the Land of the Midnight Sun.

Alaskan Roads:
Miserable or Magnificent?

It was 10 P.M. when the RVs came filing out of the bowels of the *Stardancer* into a wet, cold, foggy night. Although still daylight at this hour, the sun didn't really have its heart in it, and its feeble rays were effectively blocked by the scudding clouds and pelting rain. We picked up a heading for the town of Haines, Alaska, five miles from the debarkation dock, and trundled out into the darkness like some solemn funeral cortege.

It was not easy to get lost in a town of 1,100 people, but we managed nicely, circling around in the fog like a flock of disoriented geese, squawking our plight vociferously over our CBs. One of the few smart things we had done in preparing for the trip was to nail down reservations at a Haines campground well in advance. Now all we had to do was to find the Port Chilkoot Camper Park. Finally a joyous cry rang over the CB as one of our buddies stumbled onto the entrance to the park and guided the rest of us to its location near the center of town.

Haines is a fine place. Even in the pouring rain and marrow-chilling dampness, the warmth of the natives shone through to bask a visitor in their friendliness. Located on the upper arm of Lynn Canal, the town is the southern terminus of the Haines Highway and is a great introduction to Alaska. It was one of the Haines sourdoughs who came up with the conclusion that the seven million dollars we paid Russia for Alaska came to two cents an acre, and it still wasn't too late to hire a good lawyer and try to get our money back.

We explored the fascinating town, taking in the old fort and the Chilkat Center of the Arts, and watched Indian artisans carve their totem poles. Approaching an old Indian chiseling away on a long log, I asked him how he went about carving such beautiful sculptures. He introduced a pinch of snuff to his lower lip and nailed me with smiling eyes.

"Easy. I just cut away everything that don't look like a totem pole."

No trip to Haines is complete without visiting its outstanding state park-operated campgrounds, of which it has four within an easy drive of town. Wildlife of all types abounds, including the American bald eagles, which come here from all over Alaska to feed on the spawning salmon. And the trout and salmon fishing has been known to send an angler into fits of hypoxia. The natives may have to mush through eight feet of snow in the wintertime, but in summertime the Haines area is idyllic.

We spent hours nosing around the Sheldon Museum and Cultural Center, had a splendid meal at the old Halsingland Hotel, which once served as commandant's quarters for the fort, then all too soon it was time to untether Rocinante and head out of camp.

As if lamenting our departure, the skies once again choked up and started to bawl. As we pulled into a gas station at the edge of town, however, I noticed the wet weather failed to dampen the spirits of the Hainesites.

We had no sooner pulled up to the pump than a figure in an orange raincoat came bounding out of the station and up to the driver's window. "Ah ha," I said to the missus. "You're about to meet a real genuine sourdough—a female one, at that."

The figure that bulged the raincoat was definitely female, and the face that peered up at me from under the hood was definitely attractive. "Beautiful day," she said, wiping the dripping water from her nose. "Summer has finally arrived."

I opened the driver's door, got out, and unlocked the gas cap. "I have seen more beautiful summer days," I said, trying to blink the rain out of my eyes.

"You people from the outside just don't understand. It's summertime. Daylight until almost midnight. A little rain is great for our short growing season." She stuck the hose nozzle into the filler neck. "In the wintertime when you're in snow butt-deep to a tall giraffe, and the wind is howling eighty miles an hour—now that's bad weather. This is a beautiful summer day."

"I stand corrected. Can you tell me how to get to Haines Junction on this beautiful summer day?"

"Easy as pie," she said, pointing. "See that sign up there in the next block, with the arrow pointing left to Highway 4?"

"I do," I said, straining to see through the rain that was sheeting my glasses.

"Well, ignore that sign. Everybody follows it and ends up down at the fishing dock instead of Haines Junction, mainly on account of it was installed upside down. Have to fix it one of these days. Just turn right at the sign that says turn left. You can't go wrong."

"Thanks a bunch. How's the road to Haines Junction?"

She squeezed her brown eyes and looked at me narrowly. "You new in these parts?"

"Roger. Just off the boat."

"Then let me explain something. Roads in Alaska are not a question of road condition, but a question of mental attitude. Never ask how roads are in Alaska."

I removed my fogged glasses to squint at the young lady. "I'm not sure I understand."

"It's simple. Our roads are always under construction, due to the frost heaves and the potholes and what have you. So, as I say, it's not a matter of road condition, it's a question of mental attitude. If you're used to California freeways and think you're going to make ninety miles an hour, the roads are going to be God-awful. But if you came to Alaska to see the sights, the beautiful country, the bald eagles, and wildflowers . . . and are content to make thirty or forty miles an hour, the roads are going to be just fine."

"I think I understand what you're saying."

"Hope you do. You asked about road conditions." She tapped her temple. "It's all up here."

"I'll remember that."

"Just stop to sniff the flowers. You won't mind the roads."

I paid for the gas, shook the water off my poncho, and crawled into the driver's seat. As she brought my change, I rolled down the window for one parting remark. "Thanks for the good advice. Glad I ran into a bona-fide Alaskan at this stage of our journey."

"Bona-fide Alaskan?" she giggled. "I'm from L.A."

"L.A.? Then what are you doing in Alaska?"

"Attending the University of Alaska; psych major."

"A psych major!"

"Affirmative. This is my summer job." Her grin lit up the inside of her hood. "Thanks. And keep your powder dry."

As she ducked back into the station, I put Rocinante in gear and eased out onto the street. The distaff turned to me. "Now, about your real genuine bona-fide sourdough—"

"Just shuddup," I said. "And pour me a cup of coffee."

Laying an Egg in Chicken

As any writer will tell you, the only place as good as the local saloon to do research is the local laundromat. It is here among the steaming wash, the smell of spilled detergent, the clunk-clunk of tennis shoes spinning in the dryer that a person may collect more dirt than one disposes of.

Hankering to absorb the local color of Valdez, Alaska, during our recent RV tour, I carried the wash into a local dirty-duds mecca for the missus. In the process I almost tripped over a woman of ample proportions who was buried headfirst in one of the machines. When I excused myself, she straightened up long enough to fix me with a bloodshot stare. I was somewhat taken aback to see she was wearing a T-shirt emblazoned with the words I WAS HATCHED IN CHICKEN, ALASKA. "Were you really?" I asked timorously.

"Was I really what?" returned a voice that could harmonize with a gravel crusher.

"Hatched in Chicken, Alaska?"

"You better believe it!" With her sleeve she wiped a nose that would have felt at home on a moose. "You better believe it."

"I believe it. Where, pray tell, is Chicken, Alaska?"

"You mean you ain't never been to Chicken?"

"Afraid not."

"It's on the Taylor Highway. On the way to Dawson City. You haven't lived 'til you been to Chicken."

"Well, I'll have to remedy that. I'll certainly visit Chicken."

"The settlers were gonna call the place Ptarmigan. You know, after the state bird. But nobody knew how to spell Ptarmigan, so they called it Chicken."

"Makes sense to me."

She wrinkled her huge nose as she stuffed overalls and shirts into the washer. "Holy hogbreath! Didja ever smell anything like these grubbies? Make a polecat puke."

I decided against the sniff test. "A bit gamey?"

"You better believe it. My boyfriend's a trapper. He had to hole up in an old cabin that a big, black bear thought belonged to him. After a week the bear finally sauntered off, and my boyfriend got the hell out of there. When I got these clothes off him, I had to beat 'em with a stick to get 'em to lie down."

"Now hold it. I know this is the last frontier and all that, but if you expect me to believe a bear . . . "

She slammed the lid down on the washer. "Don't make didly squat to me whether you believe it or not. But if I was you, I wouldn't go tell my boyfriend that he didn't get cornered by a bear." She sized me up. "He's a big sucker. Make two of you."

I held up my hands in surrender. "You have my word. I'll never tell your boyfriend he wasn't cornered by a bear."

By the time my Dortha had finished the laundry, I had also met and conversed with a nice couple from Quebec who were RVing in a 34-foot Southwind, a recently divorced carpenter from Cordova who forgot to remove a ballpoint pen from his shirt pocket and wondered why all his wash was blue, and a drunk who made the mistake of making a pass at HATCHED IN CHICKEN, ALASKA and very nearly ended up rotating in the industrial dryer.

There is, indeed, no place quite like a busy laundromat to sample the local flavor. Especially in Valdez, Alaska. And now that the idea had been hatched, I knew a visit to Chicken also had to be included in our Alaskan itinerary.

It was several weeks later before we had the chance. We were advised that the road was all gravel, that gasoline stations were very sparse, and that it could be very dusty. But we had to see Chicken. So throwing all caution to the winds, we picked up the Tetlin Junction turnoff to Dawson City.

The road was washboardy with occasional deep potholes, but we throttled back to about thirty miles an hour, which was fine, for the scenery was magnificent and the traffic practically nonexistent. So adept did I become at dodging potholes, I was soon anointed the Artful Dodger by the better half.

We puffed over the summit of Mount Fairplay, and finally, blinking from the dust of a passing car, I almost missed Chicken. But I caught the turnoff in time to make it, and we wheeled off to bump up the road that led to the one street.

With a population of thirty-seven, Chicken, Alaska, does not exactly suffer from urban blight. In fact, with one restaurant, grocery, bar, and gas station, it was easy to see why our laundromat lady crowed about being hatched in Chicken— there didn't appear to be much else to do. This was debated, however, by the bartender in the tavern when I went in to inquire about getting some gas.

"Whaddaya mean there's nothin' to do in Chicken?" asked the ruddy-faced redhead with forearms that beggared tree trunks. "This place swings. This is the newer section of Chicken. You shoulda seen the old mining camp near Chicken Creek. Chicken didn't used to amount to much."

"I can see," I said, looking around the vacant tavern, "that the town has really prospered."

"Did you know they were mining gold around here several years before gold was discovered in the Klondike?"

"No, sir. I didn't know that."

He poured himself a beer. "Now they're reworking the tailings of the Chicken Hill Mine. That's why business is booming around here."

"So that's the reason. Best I lay tracks and beat the rush-hour traffic." I looked around the old Chicken Creek Saloon, at the working men's caps adorning the walls, the Chicken paraphernalia—including T-shirts more explicit than the one I had seen on the woman in Valdez. An indefinable feeling washed over me, as if I had been warped back into an earlier time. Reluctant to leave, I ordered a beer. "I guess this is about as close as one can get to the last frontier."

"Yep," said the bartender. "We still have shootouts up here, just like they did in the Old West. Other day two miners drew on each other in a dispute over a mining claim. When the smoke cleared, the less badly injured drove the other one to the hospital."

I blew the foam off my beer. "I find that hard to believe."

"Hell, another miner got ticked off at the performance of his partner's automobile, shot it full o' holes, burned it, and buried it in a tailings pile with his bulldozer. The same miner was later put in the slammer for chaining his young son to a tree and disciplining him by firing rifle shots in his direction."

"Ah, come on! You've been reading too much Louis L' Amour."

He lifted his right hand. "So help me. That's nothing. Couple of years ago a woman new to the area up here shot her husband after he brought her up to his remote nine-foot-square cabin and wouldn't let her leave. Folks up here are pretty understanding. A coroner's jury ruled it as justifiable homicide."

"Fantastic. A fella could really fall in love with Chicken, Alaska." I skoaled my beer.

As I went out the tavern's swinging door, I pushed my hat back on my head with my thumb and swaggered toward my six-wheeled steed, ready to slap leather to protect the homestead. Only a scrawny old chicken debated my right-of-way.

Mounting up and pulling out of town, it was interesting to note that Chicken may never have a smog problem, but it did have a nice little airstrip stretched out behind the saloon.

So much for the last frontier.

Alaskan Epilogue

The trip from the Canadian border back to our home in California was, needless to say, anticlimactic. We lost no time in getting Rocinante into the capable hands of Doctor Goodwrench, who hiked up her skirts to check for signs of bruised underpinnings, a leaky bladder, or splay-gaited stride.

We were overjoyed to find that, with the exception of several small lesions and a minor laceration, there was no damage to the underside of our champion. Indeed, Rocinante had weathered the ordeal like the thoroughbred she is!

Dortha toted up the meticulous expense sheet she had maintained throughout the Alaskan trip, and the results were interesting. Our journey, which had lasted exactly sixty days, ended up costing far less than we had anticipated. Camping fees had averaged four dollars a day, thanks to the many free camping spots we had encountered. Groceries, including many meals eaten out, averaged only twelve dollars a day for the two of us. We used 1,027 gallons of gasoline, including the travel from California and back. Our only other major expenses were the cost of the *Stardancer* cruise, the ferrying across Prince William Sound, and the railroad fare of the Moose Gooser between Whittier and Portage.

All told, the two-month journey through the most remote and spectacular real estate in the world had cost far less than a two-week cruise on an ocean liner for two people. A lot of vacation bang for the buck.

And now for a few lessons learned:

Would we take the trip again? You bet. Only, next time, we would probably reverse our itinerary, driving up the Alaska Highway and coming back on the *Stardancer*, or on the ferries of the Marine Highway System, thus capping off the trip with a look-forward-to bit of luxury by leaving the driving to the ship captains.

The time we selected for the trip was ideal. June through August are the ideal months to visit the Far North. This is also a good time to escape the heat of southern climes.

We should have taken along a few more spare parts for Rocinante, particularly fan belts, fuses, hoses, a spare headlight, and a little more complete tool chest than we carried. As it turned out, we were luckier than most, as we had very few problems with our new rig. Older units sometimes have a propensity to blow a radiator hose or break a fan belt out in the boondocks, miles from the nearest auto parts store. This would be even more serious were it not for the camaraderie of fellow motorhomers who, like the farmers of yesteryear, take great pride in helping one another in times of crises.

One has to approach an undertaking like this with the proper mental conditioning. Thanks to the advice tendered by old sourdoughs, we confronted this mission with the attitude that we had come to enjoy Alaska, and we would not be deterred by famine, pestilence, or disgruntled drivers. And this point cannot be overscored. By throttling back to low rpm, we found everything about the Far North exceeded our most optimistic dreams.

And the roads? As stated, these, too, are a question of attitude. There are occasional rough spots, but if taken low and slow, they present no more insurmountable problems than those in the lower states.

In summation, Dortha and I have traveled extensively both in the United States and abroad. We love to travel Europe, the Far East, South America, Canada, and, of course, our own country. In all our travels there have been none to surpass our trip to Alaska and the Canadian provinces. Particularly in a motorhome. Much of it naturally has to do with the scenery, which is unrivaled in sheer grandeur and splendor.

But just as important to the enjoyment of the Far North are its people. It takes a special breed to become Northern natives— to weather the frozen climes, the days of darkness, and the remoteness of the frozen North. And we found this special breed to be magnanimous, warm, and friendly.

Alaska is not a place to just visit. Alaska is a place to experience. One becomes imbued with its aura of vastness, its feeling of optimism and can-do among its natives, as if no challenge were too great, no vision too impossible to achieve. The completion of the Alaskan pipeline epitomizes this feeling.

Not long before this manuscript went to press, Paul Foster, our good friend in Valdez, passed away quietly in his sleep. In accordance with his wishes, he was cremated. His lovely wife, Ellen, let it be known that she would like to have his ashes scattered over his favorite fishing hole, near a waterfall in Prince William Sound. Jerry Massman, skipper of the handsome Alaskan excursion boat, the *Glacier Queen*, approached Ellen with an idea.

A short time later, Ellen was asked to be at the dock of the *Glacier Queen* with her family at a given time on a beautiful summer evening. To her surprise, the huge, 102-foot ship that can carry 167 people plus a crew of eight slid quietly from the dock with only Ellen, her family, and a few close friends aboard.

It glided silently across the sound to Paul's favorite fishing hole, where a simple but beautiful ceremony was performed under the moon-washed sky of the late summer night.

Not only had Jerry Massman provided his skippering services after an all-day trip to the Columbia Glacier and back, but the owners of Valdez's most famous excursion boat had given unqualified permission for use of the big ship for this mission of compassion.

To me, this epitomizes the spirit of big men. This epitomizes the spirit of Alaska.

Canadian Capers

We love Canada—partly because it contains so many Canadians. We never miss a chance to visit our neighbors to the north because Canada contains more than its share of characters. Case in point:

I was not expecting a female Canadian customs official, so when we pulled into the customs line in Calais, Maine, I was startled by a very comely blonde who approached Rocinante and asked to look through the motorhome. I escorted her on a short tour, making sure she saw all of our declarables. She was most pleasant, and as I showed her the bathroom, I divined that she was new on the job and had not been in too many motorhomes.

"My goodness!" she exclaimed.

"What is it?" I asked nervously.

"That water closet!"

I looked into the john, half expecting to see it full of uncut diamonds. "What's the matter with the water closet?"

"It's so tiny. I do declare, that's the smallest water closet I've ever seen!"

"I'll be happy to declare it also. I didn't know one had to declare water closets."

She smiled sweetly. "Of course, you don't have to declare water closets."

"You just did."

"That was a figure of speech. How do you manage on that tiny thing?"

I blushed. "Very well, once you get the hang of it. You sort of . . ."

"Never mind," she said, shutting the bathroom door. "You may be on your way."

I thanked her and escorted her out the door. Back in my seat, I started up Rocinante and turned to Dortha. "We forgot something."

"What, luv?"

"We forgot to get some money exchanged. Rumor has it that the rate of exchange is better on the American side."

"Let's go back to the bank in Calais. We still have a few minutes before it closes."

"We'll do it." I pulled forward, made a U-turn, and entered the return lane of the customs line. Once again I came face to face with the pretty blonde.

"Oh, it's you," she said. "It didn't take you long to see our country."

I explained the problem. She listened courteously and gave me directions to the nearest bank.

There was no place to park on the street in front of the bank, so Dortha got out and completed the transaction while I circled the block. I swooped her up on the third lap and once again headed for the customs line.

"Ah," said the blonde, sticking her head in my window for the third time "the man with the tiny plumbing."

I drew back. "Please. That's not exactly the way a fellow likes to be remembered."

"Sorry."

"Quite all right. Thanks to you, we found the bank and now, with your permission, we'll be on our way."

"You're cleared. And have a very nice vacation."

With a beginning like this, we knew we would enjoy our Canadian destination—Prince Edward Island. The Indians call this lovely island Abegweit, which means "The Home Cradled by the Waves," and it more than lives up to its billing. Rocinante cantered along the highway through the beautiful Lilliputian farms that flowered in the island's red loam, as we admired the bright colors of the farm buildings and the fertile soil that covers the finest seed potatoes in the world.

Some of the best beaches in North America are along the north shore that comprises the Prince Edward National Park. In jig time we had pulled into the park campground, had tethered Rocinante, and were toasting the sunset that was setting fire to the Gulf of St. Lawrence.

This is visiting time in the RV world, and our first visitor came in the form of an elderly gentleman who wore a trout-flied hat, a splash of red in his cheeks that shone through a thick stubble, and a twinkle in his eyes. He was bearing two huge, live lobsters.

"Hi, there," said the voice that matched the twinkling eyes. "I come bearing gifts."

"Welcome," I said, eyeing the lobsters warily.

"I'm Jacques Fry, your next-door neighbor. You like lobster?"

"We love lobster," said Dortha.

"Then I'd be obliged if you'd take these off my hands. I've eaten so damn many, I'm beginnin' to claw people."

"We'll relieve you of your crustaceans, Jacques," I said, taking the lobsters.

"I'm from Halifax, Nova Scotia," he said, seating himself. "My buddies and I come up here every year."

My wife looked at him curiously. "Your buddies? So you're not married?"

He grinned. "Of course I'm married. That's why I'm up here with my buddies. We come here and fish for two weeks. We have trout for breakfast, lobster for dinner, play poker, and let our beards grow."

"But your wives," said the missus, "what a vacation this must be for them."

"They love it more'n we do. They stay home and play bridge for two weeks straight; live on salted peanuts."

Dortha laughed. "What a vacation!"

"Don't knock it," said the stubbled cherub. "When you get to be our age, it's the best kind. I go home after looking a lobster in the face for two weeks, and the old lady looks pretty good. She's glad to see me, because I don't look like a salted peanut. Then we're good for another year. Can't beat that with a stick."

"Can't," I said, chuckling.

"Well, gotta go home and fix the roof." He rose. "Nice meetin' you."

"The roof in your motorhome?" I asked.

"The same." His rosy cheeks spread to accommodate a large grin. "Darn pressure cooker blew up last night. The gauge went right through the roof."

"Good Lord!" said the missus. "How awful!"

"More funny than awful. One of my buddies read somewhere that lobsters were good boiled in beer, so he poured in half a case." He chuckled. "Wonder we didn't blow up the whole danged campground."

In the easy camaraderie of the RV world, we were soon bosom buddies with the three fishermen next door, and the next night they invited us over for dinner.

It was a memorable evening. Everyone had to eat standing up, because the fishermen had forgotten to bring any chairs along. But before the evening was over, it's doubtful if Canadian-American relations had ever reached a higher plateau.

We hated to see the big motorhome with the patched-up roof pull out the following morning, and we waved until it tracked its erratic course down the road and out of sight.

From the pretty little blonde who had ushered us into her country to the jovial fishermen who had made our destination so enjoyable, we knew this was going to be an extra special Canadian vacation.

And it was. There was no acid rain on our parade.

The Orange Tree

As stated, the Anderson tribe has long had a love affair with Canada. Not only have we spent many RV vacations in the arms of our friendly neighbors to the north, but awhile back we traversed the complete length of Canada's main highway—good old No. 1—from St. Johns, Newfoundland, to Victoria, British Columbia.

From such a trip come many unforgettable experiences, naturally, both marvelous and maddening. Looking back on our romp across the bosom of Canada on its Maple Leaf Highway, however, one incident will never be forgotten. It concerns the wife's orange tree—a tiny memento of her home that we had uprooted to become temporary full-time axle-geese as we wended our way from our home in Virginia to take up a new life in the more hospitable climes of sunny California—via the Trans-Canada Highway.

We were clearing customs in Victoria, our last day in Canada, when we encountered a thorough customs official. Going through the motorhome with the inspector, I dutifully pointed out my rifle, TV set, Scotch, and the last-day loot the wife had purchased. The customs official only smiled the polite customs official smile—as inscrutable as a cast-iron fortune cookie—until we came to Dortha's orange tree. The polite smile broadened, and a flare went off in the blue eyes of the inspector.

"Aha!" he said, looking at the orange tree and then at me as though he had just discovered the Hope diamond concealed in my navel. "What have we here?"

"Oh that," I said, trying to act nonchalant. "That's the wife's orange tree. Now here inspector, are the papers on the rifle and the tele . . ."

"An orange tree? A bloody live orange tree?"

"Why, yes. Rather a nice one, don't you think? It was given to the missus as a farewell gift by our neighbors in Virginia. . . ."

"You're bringing in a live orange tree? From Canada?" He studied the two Ping-Pong-ball-size oranges and the three lethargic leaves that comprised the sole adornment to its spindly limbed nakedness.

"Actually, we brought it from the states through Canada. Now here's where I keep my booze and my cigarettes. . . ."

My attempts to throw up a camouflaging smoke screen were fruitless. "You know," he said, leveling his blue eyes at me, "we cannot possibly let that into the country."

"We can't?"

"Afraid not, sir."

"But that orange tree was born in the U.S. It's as American as you or I. It just wants to return to the land from which it came. I didn't know you had to have naturalization papers for an orange tree."

"The regulations are very strict and very explicit about bringing in fresh fruit and plants from Canada. Here you seem to have both."

"You are not harboring any thoughts about confiscating that orange tree?" I looked at the inspector dumbfounded.

"I'm afraid I have to, sir."

"I'm afraid you haven't met my wife."

When the missus, who had been preoccupied in the copilot's

seat, saw the customs official emerge from Rocinante with the potted orange tree in hand, I looked around for the nearest fallout shelter.

It was the first time I ever saw a customs official tackled from behind—by an irate redhead, who happened to be my wife. It got quite sticky for a considerable length of time, and we all ended up in the chief inspector's office—the customs official with a white-knuckle grip on the orange tree, the wife with a white-knuckle grip on the customs official.

"If you think for one minute," said the distaff, trying hard to keep her voice from cracking the plaster in the chief inspector's office, "that you're going to take that orange tree, you've got another think coming."

"But, madam," said the chief inspector, "our regulations are very clear on this point. I'll be glad to show them to you. . . ."

"I don't care about your damned old regulations. That tree was given to me by dear friends to plant in our new California home. It's a symbol—a symbol of a new life. I've fed and watered, and comforted this orange tree over 5,000 miles of hell and high water. . . ."

"Darling," I said, my finger to my lips, "not only are you making a scene, but you're mixing your metaphors. . . ."

"I'll do worse than mix my metaphors! I'll mix up that customs inspector if he so much as lays a hand on that orange tree! Andy, you're a man. Do something!"

I did. I perspired a lot.

The spouse finally consented to give up the orange tree on one condition. That condition being if it had to stay in Canada, she was personally going to be guaranteed that it would be properly cared for. The United States government reluctantly agreed to the proposal.

Therefore, the late-morning tourists passing through customs were startled to see a group marching from the U.S. Customs Service office over to the Canadian customs office, led by a firm-jawed redhead and a customs inspector bearing a small potted orange tree like Joseph of Arimathea might have carried the Holy Grail. A very red-faced wagon master reluctantly brought up the rear. One could almost hear the cadence beat of unseen snare drums.

It took some time before Dortha finally located a Canadian customs man who was married, had a nice home, and who promised faithfully to lay down his life before allowing any harm to befall the precious orange tree. And then, only after calling the customs official's wife and getting surprised but further guarantees of safekeeping, did the distaff give a farewell pat to the pot of the orange tree and bid the customs officials a moist farewell.

Dortha had prudently extracted visitation rights during the divorce from her orange tree. Now, years later, we plan to go back to Victoria and see how her orange tree is thriving in Canadian soil.

I would assume most botanists are of the opinion that orange trees don't do worth a hoot in Canada. If this is true, and, knowing my wife, I'll probably be the proud possessor of a brand-new Canadian hothouse—a commodity I need, needless to say, like one needs a kink in one's sewer hose.

Hell hath no fury like a redhead whose orange tree has been abducted. And if my redhead wants a Canadian hothouse, she's by-god gonna have one—providing, of course, we can get it through customs.

Pooper Cushions, Anyone?

Okay, fellow traipsers in the toolies, do you have an occasional attack of the freeway fidgets? Does your spouse sometimes have to pry your fingers off the steering wheel with a crowbar? Do you get upset just because a nearsighted station attendant filled your water tank with hi-test gasoline? Do you find yourself belting more Mylanta® than mai tais?

Then maybe it's time for an attitude check.

During nearly three decades of motorhoming, Big Red and I have worn out four Rocinantes while tilting our lances at the windmills of RV travel. And there have, indeed, been a few occasions that have sent the adrenaline into overdrive.

Like the time I drove out of the rest stop in Arizona thinking the redhead was in the rig's john and discovering sixty miles later she was back at the rest-stop dumpster. Hell hath no fury like an abandoned redhead.

Or the time I neglected to crank down the TV antenna and wiped out all the flourescent lights in the ceiling of the gas station.

Or the time I mistakenly pulled the blackwater valve on our new motorhome parked in the driveway, just as the christening party arrived.

As we all know, these little accidents do happen, adding spice to the delectable bouillabaisse of our RV world. Trick is, to keep these little faux pas from shorting tempers, double-clutching the sweat glands, and bringing on anxiety attacks—all of which can be hazardous to one's happy hour.

How do we do this? The very best thing in the world to unclench the white knuckles, to untie the stomach knots, to soothe the savage breast is, of course, a large dose of humor.

This point was underscored recently when I had open-heart surgery to install a new ticker kicker. While frolicking through post-operative recovery, an old buddy brought me a copy of Norman Cousins' *Anatomy of an Illness*. In his book, Cousins, who suffered from a crippling disease, discovered that laughter was one of the most powerful curatives that could be employed to tame an illness.

Cousins would con his nurse into pulling the shades and projecting old Marx Brothers movies on the wall of his ward. It was his contention that ten minutes of belly laughs had an anesthetic effect that would provide two hours of pain-free sleep.

Now, thanks to the new science of humor physiology known as *gelatology*, researchers have concluded that humor plays a vital role in the recovery of hospital patients. Laughter raises the pulse rate and blood pressure, which aids circulation, strengthens the heart and clears mucus from the lungs. It also does miracles for morale, the ague, and the pip.

Says Dr. Ann Kiessling of the Harvard Medical Center, "People who get a hoot out of life spend less time in the hospital. Giving vent to some belly laughs will have a most salubrious effect, especially when the hospital bill is presented."

To this end, appalled at the paucity of humor materials available to help with my recovery, I decided to sit down and write a wild, off-the-wall how-to tome designed to bring a few chortles and chuckles into the antiseptic halls of our modern hospital. Thus, my latest book, *How to Survive Hospital Care*, or *Why*

They Keep Bedpans in the Freezer, was born. I will undoubtedly be sued by every doctor and hospital on the continent.

A great deal of research has gone into the book, which has unearthed many secrets that hospitals would rather you didn't know. Such as the fact that all hospital food is designed around a product loosely described as gelatin. Actually, this dish of translucent latex is produced by the Goodyear Tire and Rubber Company under a contract dating back to the Civil War.

Although possessing no nutritional value, and having all the sapidity attraction of rubber cement, gelatin has one quality that has long endeared it to the medical community: It is impossible to spill. Whereas just about anything else will slop over on its journey from scullery to sick bay, gelatin will not. Indeed, it can be dribbled down the hall and slam-dunked into a patient's tray without so much as missing a quiver. Its one redeeming quality is that it doesn't have to be mopped up.

Another little known fact is the reason hospital nurses take so much blood during a patient's visit. Administrators would rather you didn't know that hospitals defray spiraling medical expenses by selling bat guano to kumquat growers. Which explains why you will find bat caves in the basement of most hospitals. Unfortunately, bats are voracious little critters and must be fed half a dozen times a day. And since bats like human blood, you now know why veins must be poked on an hourly basis.

The above items are just a few of the fascinating disclosures in *How to Survive Hospital Care*, Legendary Publishing, (800) 358-1929, which contains such exciting chapters as "Romancing Your Bedpan," "Should You Have Sex During Surgery?" and "Be Leery of Surgeons Bearing Chain Saws." All of which may be instrumental in mending a fractured funny bone.

In case this reads like a plug for a new book, that's only because it is. The usual author royalties accruing from the book bought by readers of this tome (who identify themselves as such) will be donated to the very worthwhile Dogs for the Deaf program.

This most laudatory project, which provides free dogs trained to act as ears for the hearing impaired, has long been endorsed and supported by the Good Sam Club and its various chapters.

So, as Happy Harry Motorhome Owner, will adding more humor in your life help with your occasional heartburn or stress tic? Should you dash right out and buy a pooper cushion and a dribble glass? If it will light up your life, why not? The most important and healthy thing to do is tickle your fancy and flex your funny bone.

As Norman Cousins said, "Humor saved my life." Humorists Dave Barry and Erma Bombeck are proof that fun is the best medicine. When apprised of our new book, Barry, whose lively off-center view of life has helped him through a recent divorce, took time to wish me luck with *How to Survive Hospital Care.*

The late Erma Bombeck, whose marvelous homespun humor helped her face her dialysis machine, said, "I'm delighted you are still doing your part to bring some laughter into a world that sorely needs it."

So, there you have it, fellow vagabonds. On those rare occasions when we get the motorhome misgivings or closet claustrophobia, let's relax with a little more humor in our daily lives.

If you don't believe humor can put a gleam in your eye and have a salubrious effect on your longevity, remember a certain gent who was an authority on the subject. His name was George Burns.

Colorful, Congenial, Classy Colorado

B ack in the Stone Age, when I was knee-high to a toadstool, we lived in a fly-speck of a town called Sargents, Colorado. My dad was the manager of a lumber company, and we lived in a thirteen-room log cabin containing the first flushing toilet in the county. Unfortunately, the toilet was installed before we had either running water or sewage disposal.

We hated to see company come, because one of us siblings had to carry buckets of water to fill the cistern in the attic so Dad could show off the flushing toilet. Needless to say, the basement got pretty ripe before Dad finally got around to installing a septic tank.

These cherished memories came flooding back when we recently revisited the highest state in the nation. Colorado has got to be one of the most beautiful hunks of terra firma on this planet, as attested to by Katharine Lee Bates when she looked out upon the majesty of Pikes Peak and wrote a ditty called "America the Beautiful."

Although Colorado is jam-packed with splendor, space permits only the mention of two of our favorite off ramps—both off Interstate 25, which bisects the Centennial State. The first is one of our favorite cities: Boulder, Colorado.

There being not too many metropolises that own their own glacier from which they pipe in their water, it has been fascinating to watch this sleepy little college town blossom into one of the leading educational and research centers in the Rocky Mountains, not the least of which is the National Center for Atmospheric Research, a great place to visit if you have a thing for solar flares.

This mile-high city has not grown too big for its britches, however, and still maintains an idyllic, rustic charm—very well represented by its 8,500 acres of mountain parks, including Boulder Creek Path, which nuzzles the creek as it meanders through the prettiest parts of town.

The main reason the Boulder off ramp must be taken is because a visit to the Leanin' Tree Museum of Western Art is an absolute must. This is the headquarters of the world's largest publisher of Western and wildlife greeting cards, and one whole wing has been devoted to one of the largest privately owned collections of Western art in the country.

I first met Ed Trumble, founder of the Leanin' Tree and curator of this magnificent museum, some years back when he had acquired the rights to make greeting cards from Norman Rockwell's *Saturday Evening Post* covers. He had asked me to write the greeting-card messages that would accompany the illustrations. Needless to say, to a struggling young word-cruncher, this was a most prestigious assignment, and we had a blast trying to do justice to one of America's greatest artists.

Today, Ed Trumble is a fine figure of a man. He has kept himself as fit and trim as a hungry cowpoke, and he takes great delight in conducting personal tours of his outstanding display of Western Americana. A guy, who made a gazillion dollars publishing a greeting card that shows an old, grinning, snaggletoothed cowhand saying: "I spent most of my money on beer and women. The rest I just wasted," can't be all bad.

The museum parking lot will accommodate RVs, which are cordially welcomed. For Western art lovers, this off ramp leads to a visitation that will truly jangle your spurs. Say Andy sent you, and if Ed is not swamped, you'll have an opportunity to shake hands with the man who has been a benefactor to more Western artists, landscapists, and sculptors than you can shake a cattle prod at.

Our favorite second Colorado off ramp takes us to the bustling vacation spot at the foot of Pikes Peak: Colorado Springs. At one time, thanks to gold and silver strikes, this burgeoning community was touted as having more millionaires per capita than any city in the United States. Many scions of the English gentry arrived, and polo, riding to the hounds, and having high tea became so much a part of the Springs that it soon bore the shibboleth of Little London.

One may still browse through the Broadmoor Hotel, a world-class resort, for a touch of the elegance of yesteryears. This tribute to decorum and good taste has no less than nine outstanding dining rooms.

Something for everyone, the Springs boasts marvelous zoos, museums, and art centers galore; the Garden of the Gods is unique, with its towering red sandstone formations that include such visual delights as Balanced Rock and the Kissing Camels. Other attractions are the Pro Rodeo Hall of Fame, depicting the history of rodeo and its champions; the World Figure Skating Museum Hall of Fame, honoring international skaters such as Sonja Henie and Peggy Fleming; and the U.S. Olympic Complex, where Olympic hopefuls are trained. More than 15,000 athletes annually attend this training center, which also houses the national headquarters for the U.S. Olympic Committee. All of these functions are open to visitors.

A number of military installations reside in the Colorado Springs area. One of the most fascinating is the North American Air Defense Command (NORAD), which lies in a chunk of hollowed-out granite known as Cheyenne Mountain. Hopefully impervious to aerial attack, NORAD was command-central for our American troops during the Desert Storm conflict.

Check in at Peterson Air Force Base for an excellent museum, as well as presentations on NORAD and the Air Space Command, which not only keeps track of all the space missions and junk floating in space, but also lets the little ankle biters know when Santa's sleigh is entering the galaxy.

Highest on the must-see list is the Air Force Academy. Even the little lady will enjoy this, as the noon formation parade of 4,000 crew-cutted, flat-gutted, handsome young men and women heading for chow in lock-step precision is guaranteed to make the chest buttons pop.

Rumor has it that the cadets once worked out a plan to flush all the dormitory toilets at the same time, to see how high the hydraulic surge would blow up the parade-ground fireplug. It was my great pleasure to know former Superintendent of the Air Force Academy Lieutenant General Thomas S. Moorman, and he denied the story.

By all means, cruise through the academy grounds, take time to watch the glider pilots and parachute jumpers, and don't leave without visiting the academy chapel. This magnificent edifice with its seventeen spires stabbing the blue Colorado sky (dubbed the paratrooper's nightmare by the cadets) is understandably Colorado's leading tourist attraction.

Just watch out for deer as—believe it or not—a couple dozen are killed on the academy roads every year.

RVers should earmark a couple of weeks to visit these two fascinating locales. When seeing Boulder, contact the Boulder

Visitors Bureau, 2440 Pearl Street, Boulder, Colorado 80302; (303) 442-2911.

Goodies galore await you at the Colorado Springs Tourist Bureau at 104 S. Cascade, Suite 104, Colorado Springs, Colorado 80903; (800) DO VISIT. Both of these excellent welcome centers will provide maps, events schedules, and info on where to park your rig.

As you readers know, Rocinante, our rubber-shod steed, has a mind of her own. When moseying through Colorado, she always gallops off on these two off ramps. We'll meet you there and toast that beautiful Colorado sunset.

Christmas in Beantown

She may be a couple eggs short in her waffle batter, but she is an attractive, ingratiating young lady who loves life and bites it off in huge chunks. She was supposed to have been a boy, but when she appeared with different plumbing, her name was changed from Andrew to Ann Drue. In spite of her idiosyncrasies, we couldn't love Ann more if she were our own daughter, which she happens to be.

As a biochemist, Ann loves to study nature, which accounts for the fact that she has four kids, a donkey, seven goats, a cranky cat, a splay-gaited basset hound, gerbils, frogs, and a husband with a very nervous tic.

All of which is fine, except when Ann accepted a job at Harvard, she insisted on taking her whole menagerie to Boston with her. Only problem, she was living in Portland, Oregon, at the time.

Even this would have been of small moment had she not shipped the cat and the dog in the same airline container, and had not the issue with old Doc arisen.

The airline brouhaha began with a harried reservation clerk when Ann first telephoned. "I want to know how much you'd charge to haul my ass to Boston."

There was a bit of confusion on the other end of the line before this was all straightened out, and Ann was told that the donkey would have to be crated. This was arranged, and Doc was duly delivered to the terminal, less than euphoric about being straight-jacketed in a wooden kimono.

Taking one look at the crate that was slightly smaller than Noah's ark, the airline official decided he had seriously underbid the shipping fee and made the mistake of informing Ann the fee would have to be doubled. Not one to take contract-breaching lying down, Ann told him this was exorbitant, and to just keep the donkey. About this time old Doc, feeling his oats, proceeded to vent his opinion about life in general and airline terminals in particular. The airline officialdom hastily decided that the quote they had given Ann was not such a bad deal when the alternative was pondered. Doc was duly delivered at the quoted price.

All of which brought us to Boston for the Christmas holidays, and a scouting of the beautiful country lanes and market roads of this fascinating locale, which Ralph Waldo Emerson claimed was laid out by a cow.

Ah, Beantown! Home of Tip O'Neal, the Red Sox, Beacon Hill, Paul Revere, and a delicious beer named Samuel Adams. Indeed, had not the beer barrels run dry on the *Mayflower*, Boston may have yet to be settled. For according to a *Mayflower* passenger, they were heading for Virginia when they ran out of beer: "We came to this resolution, to go presently ashore . . . our victuals being much spent, especially, our Beere." Else this fascinating city might have ended up in Virginia instead of Massachusetts.

And fascinating it is. Since the Boston Tea Party, it has been literally steeped in history and recognized as the spot that precipitated the American Revolution. And to the natives' credit, they have painstakingly preserved and restored its charm and fascinating scenic highlights.

The best way to see Boston proper is to plug your rig into one of the many excellent Boston-area RV parks listed in your handy *Trailer Life Campground/RV Park & Services Directory*, and take a bus or the efficient Metropolitan Transit Authority to downtown. Boston's ulcerating traffic can be largely avoided by taking a walk on the Freedom Trail, which winds through various neighborhoods that characterize the city: the Italian neighborhood in the North End, the "Old Boston" neighborhood at Beacon Hill, and the Irish community in Charleston.

A walking map of the Freedom Trail may be picked up at the visitor's center and embraces such historical spots as the King Chapel and Burying Ground, the Boston Massacre Site, the Paul Revere House, the Bunker Hill Monument and the USS *Constitution*—not to be missed. Our favorite is the Granary Burying Grounds which was established in 1660, and where such luminaries as Samuel Adams, John Hancock, Paul Revere, and victims of the Boston massacre rest on their laurels.

By all means the flavor of downtown Boston must be savored. But for us, the equally memorable parts of the Boston environs are our favorites—the byways and back roads.

For these, uncork your dinghy, for driving around the suburbs of Boston is not all that difficult. Ann lives in Bedford, some twenty miles outside the city center, and this was an excellent base from which to explore the many famous sites abounding in Boston's suburbs.

One can spend months soaking up the history of this cradle of democracy, but on our Christmas vacation we had to settle for some of the high spots: Walden's Pond, near Concord, the source for Thoreau's masterpiece; the marvelous whaling museum at New Bedford; and the North Bridge, where the first engagement of the Revolution took place, culminating in "the shot heard around the world."

As a sop to the little women in our family, we had to scout out the nearby home of Louisa May Alcott. And a trip to the bewitching city of Salem with its witch's museum, and the House of Seven Gables, which inspired Nathaniel Hawthorne's novel, were not to be missed.

Boston is renown not only for its blue-ribbon beer, but its culinary concoctions. We attended clambakes, sampled the legendary restaurants, had a lager at the Bull and Finch pub (better known as the setting for the *Cheers* TV series), and ate lobster until we started growing claws. Whoever invented the lobster roll should be knighted by Julia Child.

At Christmas time, Boston and its suburbs really come to life. With lights, music, and old family traditions, Bostonians relive the customs started by the colonists some 300 years ago. Christmas Eve is an especially busy time for the Cooper family, as Ann's menagerie is pressed into service.

Every year the neat little church a few blocks away erects a crèche— not a crèche with fabricated figures, but a manger with a real Joseph and Mary and live animals from Ann's zoo. Dortha and I were privileged to join the annual procession from her house, entailing a couple goats, several kids, and ole Doc, the donkey. At the head of our procession was Geof, his full white beard and his deep, professorial voice having no problem parting the waves of traffic that had gathered in front of the church.

It was a church service unlike any other in Massachusetts, marred only slightly when ole Doc joined in by braying with the bell-ringers, and Sir Galahad, one of the young goats, ate the crib of baby Jesus.

All in all, there never was a finer Christmas. And even had we not basked in the warmth of family, we will return to Boston again just to bask in the cultural, gastronomical, and historical virtues of this great city.

Is Your Hindsight 20/20?

I guess it all started when I was a young pup growing up in the wilds of Colorado during the Depression. As the old narrow-gauge train clattered down the tracks of the Denver & Rio Grande Railroad, my big brother used to throw rocks at the locomotive fireman. The fireman responded by throwing coal at my brother and me.

Then when the caboose went by, we'd pick up the coal and take it home in our wagon to stoke the kitchen stove.

This may, or may not, have planted the psychological seed that has made me enamored of cabooses. And rear ends. There is something about the derrières of life that I find fascinating.

If one studies the rear ends of RVs, one can very easily divine the personality of the vehicle's owner. As a long-time student of RV backsides, I have spent much time and effort in diagnosing the personality traits of our fellow happy campers, just by observing the area surrounding the rear license plate. For instance:

Many RVers like to advertise their names, CB handles, and monitoring channels on the backs of their rigs. Such a sign might read: "Cora and Cecil Appleby, Beaumont, Texas. Handle's Apple Cora. Monitor Channel 13. Y'all give a call, ya hear?"

Obviously, these folks are outgoing, gregarious types who like to chat with fellow nomads as they browse the byways.

This is the camper crew you like to encounter on a remote section of the Alcan Highway, where friendly neighbors are few and far between.

Also in the Type "A" category are the RVers who emblazon the rears of their rigs with maps of the United States, with the various states they have visited outlined. Here again, we know these vagabonds are warm, outgoing, chatty folks who are interested in seeing the United States and who invite other nomads to share adventures with them.

They are nice people to encounter when you discover your copilot wrapped the fish heads in your only map and disposed of them in a dumpster thirty miles back. These people always have a full map file, as they have either visited, or intend to visit, every state in the Union.

The big, beautiful diesel pusher with the wild leopard painted on the rear? This signifies that the owners are obviously in the higher-income bracket, probably retired, and like to camp out and rough it as long as the ice maker in the wet bar doesn't screw up. They are generally very intelligent, gracious, and well-informed, or they would not have made a megazillion bucks to spend on an RV. These are also great people to camp by in remote areas, as they often have a wide-screen television with a satellite dish that will pick up Outer Mongolia and if properly approached might even let you use their Jacuzzi.

Among the many personality traits that are manifested on the behind of one's rig these days are, of course, bumper stickers. These run the gamut from the old classic, "If This Rig's Rockin' Don't Bother Knockin'"—obviously displayed by newlyweds—to the venerable logo of the old-timers, "Please Don't Dent Our Children's Inheritance."

Indeed, a writer by the name of Carol Gardner has recently scribed a whole book titled *Bumper Sticker Wisdom—America's*

Pulpit Above the Tailpipe. This collection of mini-interviews seeks to answer the question of what motivates such bumper art as "So Many Pedestrians . . . So Little Time," and "Happiness Is Seeing Your Boss's Picture on the Back of a Milk Carton."

According to the *Los Angeles Times,* Gardner, aged fifty, is a veritable bumper-sticker scholar. She roams around the countryside—from a Mosquito Festival in Paisley, Oregon, to the World Champion Cow-Chip Throwing Contest in Beaver, Oklahoma—collecting eclectic information about America's fender philosophers.

My favorite chrome-wrapper is "If Reindeer Really Can Fly . . . Our Windshields Are in Big Trouble." Probably the less said about bumper adornments the better, but they do tend to shape ideas about the RV occupants. Especially when a rear end is festooned with the driver's ideas about gun control, politics, abortion, and religion—any of which are guaranteed to trigger debates more heated than the campfire.

In Wyoming, we recently encountered a van with a bumper sticker that read "My Son's an Honor Student." Not to be outdone, a gunracked camper later passed us sporting the decal: "My Kid Can Whup Your Honor Student." We fervently hoped the two RVers didn't end up sharing the same campground.

Hind ends that support bicycle racks, mopeds, skimobiles, or folding kayaks are often de rigueur and should be approached with caution. Owners of such muscle-testing devices are generally in great shape, exude good cheer, like to slap people on the back a lot, and drink cranberry juice during happy hour.

A recent vogue is gaily decorated tire covers for rigs carrying their spares on their behinds. We once decorated a tire cover to publicize a new book I had written: *Home Sweet Home Has Wheels.* We didn't sell any books, but we got dozens of offers to buy the tire cover.

An interesting report comes from a driver from Clearwater, Florida, who had a tire cover on the back of his Flair motorhome that read, "If your spouse was in the mood last night, give a grin."

"I've gotta remove that cover," said the Floridian. "So many people pass me grinning and chuckling they almost run off the road."

Says a fulltimer from Bangor, Maine, "I finally solved the problem of people who like to tailgate. On the rear of my Winnie I rigged up this red neon sign that blinks. When someone insists on dogging my tail, I switch it on. It reads RADIOACTIVE MATERIAL—DO NOT COME WITHIN 50 FEET." He grinned. "You should hear the brakes squeal."

And, of course, no self-respecting rear end would ever be seen in public without sporting the grinning logo of the Good Sam Club. Our haloed camper signifies that its rig's owners are not only sociable and good neighbors but are more than willing to lend a helping hand during an emergency.

In view of the above, it is very apparent that our posterior tells more about us than we realize. It might be prudent to check it out occasionally.

At least that's what my adorable spouse, Big Red, did. She recently came lugging home two videos. We now spend Saturday nights watching *You Too Can Have Buns of Steel* and *How to Have a Gorgeous Gluteus Maximus.*

This summer, our rear ends are going to be in great shape. I hope we can say the same for our rig.

May your hindsight be equally as rewarding.

Rocinante the Third

Well, we went and did it. Actually, there was no choice. Rocinante the Second's holding tanks were full, her propane and gas tanks were empty. Furthermore, a rear spring had lost a bout with a bad pothole in a Baja road, and at low speeds the gallant steed had developed a painful waddle—sort of like an old layer hen with a broken egg bag. Rocinante the Second had chalked up a lot of miles. It was time to either shoot her or put her on the auction block. Dortha insisted on pursuing the latter option, naturally.

After I had all of her ailments taken care of, we put the Southwind up for sale. Thanks to Dortha's meticulous care and feeding of her charge, the first couple who saw Rocinante the Second bought her. They promised her a good home and guaranteed us visitation rights. We watched our old friend disappear down the street in the hands of strangers, while Dortha puddled a box of Kleenex.

Now came the big question. In today's dizzying motorhome market, what would become Rocinante the Third? As veteran RVers, the distaff and I had learned long ago that if one plans to do more sitting than traveling, one should have a larger RV. If one opts for more traveling than sitting, a smaller motorhome can be more practical. That's why Rocinante the First was a 30-foot Apollo, a large rig for the 1970s; we had planned to spend a lot of time parked while we explored this great country of ours. It had worked out beautifully.

But the call of the wilds beckoned, and we found ourselves planning extensive trips to Alaska and Mexico. In deference to crowded ferries in Alaska and railroad flatcars in Mexico, we had sold our Apollo and bought a sprightly 24-foot Southwind. The smaller rig was naturally peppier, could frolic easily over the washboard roads of our neighboring countries, and could fit nicely into any campground. Since we were on the move and spending much of our time outside, the closer confines of the rig were not a problem. Rocinante the Second was a loyal, cost-effective, and lovable beast; she fulfilled her mission like the thoroughbred she was.

But our RVing mode had once again changed, and we planned to do as much sitting as driving. So we decided on a compromise between the two: a motorhome in the 28-foot range.

Now for the big decision: What kind of a 28-foot rig to buy? We haunted every RV show within 500 miles, exploring the dazzling array of handsome new motorhomes. Finally, by the process of elimination, we narrowed down the choice to several makes that offered what we wanted: a rear bedroom with twin beds, and a forward divan so we could both watch the evening news on the boob tube in comfort. I insisted on the Chevy chassis, only because the old 454-engine has been around long enough to get most of the bugs out, and it had served us well in more than 100,000 miles of motorhoming.

We toyed with the idea of a basement model but decided against it for several reasons. We had always found the storage space in our conventional RV more than adequate, and since we were moving to Boise, Idaho, and planned on doing a lot of camping in the boonies, we did not want that extra height to contend with when snaking through the virginal forests. Being scraped by branches is one thing, but being scraped by tree limbs can be downright dangerous to one's rooftop air-conditioner.

Also, I had done my homework and knew that some of the basement models had gross vehicle weight ratings that would allow most of the basement storage area to be filled up only if one were hauling Ping-Pong balls. This fact was underscored when we encountered a rock hound just outside of Quartzsite, Arizona. Far more knowledgeable about rare rocks than about proper load and balance of RVs, the lapidarist had filled his basement storage to the brim with rocks to take to the gem show. The basement model had been quickly transformed into a spud-cellar model, resting about a foot underground on top of a broken rear axle.

We had now winnowed down the choice to a couple of medium-price units that I thought we could afford without Dortha having to take in laundry. I turned over the final selection to her, as she is the one in the family who has good taste in everything but husbands. Somewhat to my surprise, she decided she liked the decor and the galley arrangement best in a motorhome called the Dolphin. Her decision was buttressed by the fact that our neighbors had just returned from Alaska in a new Dolphin and had experienced virtually no problems.

I called the manager of the Dolphin plant, an affable gent by the name of Lou Howard, and told him I was interested in his product, wanted to meet the president of the company, take a tour of the factory (oddly enough, many RV manufacturers discourage plant tours), and pick up a rig at the factory. Howard was most cooperative, answering yes to all the above. I then arranged financing through Good Sam's excellent financing department (better terms than those of my bank and credit union), signed with the RV dealer, and Big Red and I were off to the swinging hamlet of Perris, California, to pick up our new rig.

True to his word, Howard had our new RV ready upon our arrival, its freshly waxed fiberglass tossing back the rays of the late afternoon sun, its Michelin tires pawing at the curb like a great Percheron. That afternoon we toured the plant, becoming very impressed with the efficiency and quality of materials that went into the assembly-line production.

They let us sleep in their full hookup customer parking lot that night, and the next morning we were off in the new rig for a shakedown cruise. We planned to gallop around Arizona a bit, then toot on up to Tucson and Green Valley to visit old friends, returning to Perris, where we would have the motorhome's bugs taken care of.

We dutifully completed the 1,000-mile journey and checked back into the Dolphin plant with the list of repairs that needed to be done to the new rig. Used to having at least a couple dozen write-ups after the initial shakedown cruise, I was amazed to present the service manager with only two complaints: a tiny piece of molding that had come unglued and sporadically working windshield wipers. I was chagrined to find out that the wipers were not malfunctioning; it was the new owner, who had not finished reading the operating manual. Under the embarrassing tutelage of a serviceman, I was taught how to turn on the wipers so they would slap-slap like wipers are supposed to.

That afternoon we met with the president of the company, a slender, good-looking fellow named Wayne Mertes. I told him that we were very impressed with our new Dolphin, and I was amazed at the paucity of write-ups following our shakedown cruise.

"We can thank the amnesty program for that," he said.

I blinked at him. "The amnesty program?"

"Right. Nearly all California RV manufacturers employ a

lot of Mexican workers. In the old days, in spite of our best efforts, many of them were illegal aliens. Every time an immigration man would show up, half the work force would take off. It's difficult to maintain good quality control when half your work force is hiding in the toolies."

"I can understand that."

"Now, with the amnesty program, we have nothing but documented workers in our plant. It sure has been a boon to quality control in RV manufacturing."

"I'd never have attributed quality control to the amnesty program," I said.

"There's another angle that is interesting. We're selling our mini motorhomes to the Japanese."

"No kidding."

Mertes nodded. "We import their Toyota chassis, put our mini motorhome on it, and sell it back to the Japanese. If motorhoming takes off over there like it has here, we just might make a contribution to our deficit trade balance."

Needless to say, I was impressed. We are very pleased with Rocinante the Third. And I'm sure that if Don Quixote could see the modern namesake of his splay-gaited steed, he would be impressed, too.

Once again it's time for a christening: Rocinante the Third. And in the process, we just might raise our cups to the amnesty program.

It's Déjà Vu
All Over Again

Classy writers like to sprinkle their prose with juicy gems from such sages as Aristotle, Cato, and Confucious. This, of course, is dumb because, as everyone knows, the world's greatest philosopher was Yogi Berra. Who else ever came up with such words for a motorhomer to live by as: "When you come to a crossroads, take it," "The reason no one comes here is because it's too crowded," and, my favorite, "It's *déjà vu* all over again." And it's Yogi's *déjà vu* that inspired this chapter.

On a recent trip to California, we took the off ramp leading to the nice little city of Santa Rosa for a visit with our son, Scott, his pretty wife, Candyce, and their twin ankle biters—a safari not to be undertaken lightly.

As has been mentioned, Big Red and I have long held the opinion that children should never be allowed in the house. This goes double for twins. Scott never heeded this advice, and now not only do they get up on the furniture, but their home is awash in teddy bears, bubble gum, and half-chewed Legos, and their kitchen is decorated in early pablum. Other than that, they are great parents.

As we sat out on the patio, watching a couple chickens burning on the barby, I was astounded to hear Scott say, "You won't believe this, Dad, but I can't wait until the twins are a little older. I want to get an RV."

I choked on my sarsaparilla. "Hold it right there, son. You and your siblings never had a nice thing to say about our travel trailer when you were kids."

"Not true, Dad. I'll never forget when you put me in charge of the key to the sewer hose. It was the highlight of my life. I want my kids to have the same experience."

It wasn't until weeks later when we had returned home that I recalled what Scott had said. I looked it up in my notes for a book I had written about traveling across the newly opened Trans-Canada Highway in a Shasta trailer. I had taken a break from my military duties at Fort Fumble—as we lovingly called the Pentagon—to spend some time with my neglected family, and Dortha and I were now enjoying a vacation in our first travel trailer, dubbed "The Two-ton Albatross," with our young progeny.

If nothing else, the military teaches organization. In no time we had the hookup-and-trailer-preparation process refined to an exact science. I had prepared checklists outlining duties for everyone, and immediately after breakfast each of the troops performed his or her assigned chores.

While Dortha did the breakfast dishes, secured the breakables in the icebox, wrapped the stove grates in dish towels, and stowed them in one of the twin sinks, daughter Holly performed her ritual. This involved shutting all the windows, cranking down the ventilators, folding up her bed (which was part of the kitchen table), and stowing the blankets under the dinette benches. Her last job was to put a plastic cover over the goldfish bowl and pack it into the other twin sink along with Dortha's miniature orange tree, both of the latter having been wished on us by well-meaning friends whose collective heads I hoped someday to have on a pike.

As this feverish activity was being performed inside the trailer, young Scott flushed out the sewer hose and placed it in the hollow trailer bumper, unplugged the electrical cord and water hose, removed the jacks from under the frame, packed everything into the storage compartment, and shoved in the step under the front door.

It was my job to back the car up to the trailer, engage the ball joint, plug in the electrical wiring, level the trailer and connect the automatic stopping device. Then, with Scott's help, I checked the turn signals, trailer-brake, and running lights, and we were ready to roll.

In the Pentagon, for such well-organized administration, I would have been called a superb planner. In the trailer, I was called by my offspring such names as Simon Legree, Captain Bligh, and Der Kommandant. The fact remains, however, that with such well-oiled teamwork we could get our rig under way within twenty minutes after the second cup of morning coffee.

This particular morning was highlighted by an auspicious occasion. Due to Scott's unstinting attention to detail and devotion to the mission above and beyond the pale, the chief of staff and I had arranged a little presentation. After we had completed the hookup and were ready to travel, I mustered all hands by the trailer, and Holly read the citation. When she finished, Scott stood proudly at attention while the missus stepped forward and hung a ribboned key around his neck. Then she kissed him on both checks.

"Congratulations," she said, swallowing hard. "It's not everyone who gets the title of sanitation engineer so early in life."

"And with your own key to the closet that contains the sewer-hose connection," added Holly.

"Wear it proudly, son," I said, shaking his hand. "You have earned it."

"I—I don't know what to say," said Scott, choked with emotion. "My very own sewer key."

I cleared my throat. "Company dismissed!"

And so it was with proud heart and shining eyes that we mounted up for the mission that was to take us through the new Trans-Canada Highway on one of our greatest adventures.

Rereading those notes, I swallowed a large lump as I harkened back to the days when our kids were young, wide-eyed, and bushy-tailed. I was even glad that we had let them in the trailer.

Now, for the first time, I realized what an impression our early RV travels had had on our get; how they had registered so favorably that Scott decided he would like to do the same thing with his kids.

What makes this all so interesting is that RVing—which we considered a new and bold adventure in our day—has become firmly implanted in the new generation. Whereas we oldsters ventured out onto potholed roads that sorely tested our breadbox rigs, our baby boomers will tackle the freeways with their families in splendor we never dreamed of.

But whether driving a rig containing an ice chest and a camp stove or driving a diesel containing an ice maker and a microwave oven, the thrill of striking out on unknown adventures and testing new horizons is proving every bit as strong in the new generation as it was in ours.

RVing, especially motorhoming, has truly come of age when it passes from one generation to the next. No longer just a fad or an experiment, the thrill of the high road has become an accepted way of life and a very important part of today's human experience.

It's my fondest hope to be invited to attend the ceremony when Scott presents his son with his very own sewer key. It will have come full circle, and Big Red and I could not be more delighted.

Yogi Berra really smacked the tack on the head when he said, "It's *déjà vu* all over again."

Let's lift a jar to Yogi.

Other Books by Trailer Life

Full-time RVing: A Complete Guide to Life on the Open Road, Second Edition
Bill and Jan Moeller
This best-selling how-to-do-it book covers a broad range of subjects of interest to fulltimers, those considering a full-time lifestyle, or seasonal RVers. New and expanded chapters include working fulltimers, remodeling your RV for full-time living, and widebody RVs, in addition to chapters on costs, choosing the right RV, safety and security, and much more.
7⅜ × 9¼, 488 pages
$29.95 ISBN 0-934798-53-2
Available March, 1998

State Residency Requirements: Selecting an RV Home Base
Compiled by Martha Weiler
This annual publication is aimed at RV owners who are now living or are planning to live in their rigs year-round. These people have the freedom of selecting any state as their "home base." To help in the selection process, this booklet contains resident, income, and sales-tax responsibilities, driver's licensing, vehicle registration fees and requirements, and voter requirements.
5½ × 8½, 48 pages
$5.95 ISBN 0-934798-48-6

Trailer Life's RV Repair & Maintenance Manual, Third Edition
Edited by Bob Livingston
This newly revised edition presents recreational vehicle owners with all the practical knowledge needed for diagnosing problems, making repairs, and communicating with mechanics. Detailed troubleshooting guides for all RV systems, hundreds of comprehensive illustrations and photographs, and step-by-step instructions for repairing, replacing, and maintaining systems.
8½ × 11, 368 pages
$34.95 ISBN 0-934798-45-1

Trailer Life's Towing Guide
The editors of *Trailer Life*
This annual publication lists the last five years of tow ratings for passenger cars, light trucks, and sport-utility vehicles with factory tow ratings of 2,000 pounds or greater. Also included are listings of towable cars and of motorhome chassis manufacturers' specifications.
7⅜ × 9¼, 80 pages
$7.95 ISBN: 0-934798-47-8

The Best of Tech Topics
Bob Livingston
Over the years, thousands of RVers have corresponded with Bob Livingston through his monthly "Tech Topics" column in *Highways* magazine. *The Best of Tech Topics* includes their most important questions along with no-nonsense answers. solutions to pressing RV problems, and sources for hard-to-find accessories and replacement parts.
5½ × 8½, 112 pages
$12.95 ISBN: 0-93478-55-9

Surviving the First 24 Hours in Your RV
Bob Livingston
This is a comprehensive instruction manual designed to indoctrinate the new RV owner or renter into the world of RVing by walking the reader through the complete operation of a motorhome, travel trailer, fifth-wheel, tent trailer, or pickup camper. Systems, appliances, and accessories are described in easy-to-understand terms. Step-by-step instructions for proper operation are also included.
7⅞ × 9¼, 128 pages
$12.95 ISBN: 0-93478-46-X

100 Miles Around Yellowstone Park
Jim and Madonna Zumbo
This new book is a comprehensive guide that focuses on the sights and activities within a 100-mile radius of Yellowstone National Park. It is a valuable guide for travelers who choose Yellowstone as their destination, but don't want to miss out on the many sights and activities nearby. Particular emphasis is made on RV travel and information in this area.
6 × 9, 288 pages
$17.95 ISBN: 0-93478-52-4

These books are available at fine bookstores everywhere. Or, you may order directly from Trailer Life Books. For each book ordered, simply send us the name of the book, the price, plus $3 per book for shipping and handling (California residents please add 7.25% sales tax and Indiana 5%).

Mail to:

Trailer Life Books, 64 Inverness Drive East, Englewood, CO 80112

You may call our customer-service representatives if you wish to charge your order or if you want more information. Please phone, toll-free, Monday through Friday, 6:30 A.M. to 6:30 P.M.; Saturday, 7:30 A.M. to 1:30 P.M., Mountain Time, 1 (800) 766-1674.